A
Spiritual Tool Kit

Kathleen Pasley

"In today's chaotic world, the journey inward is not a luxury, it's a necessity."

Table of Contents

DEDICATION

Julie Saunders

In you, I found a soul sister, dearest friend and guiding light.

Thank you for walking beside me on my spiritual journey.

I look forward to seeing you on the other side.

This offering is as much yours as it is mine.

Picture of Julie and Kathleen

Photo by Igor Vynnytsky

INTRODUCTION

"As human beings, our greatness lies not so much in being able to remake the world... as in being able to remake ourselves."

- Mahatma Gandhi

I have to admit, I had a VERY unusual introduction to spirituality. In fact, I completely stumbled into a spiritual life. Close to 40 years ago, I was on a business trip to Los Angeles. I was in a high-powered and intense job at the time, and I wasn't in the least bit interested in spirituality. In fact, I was so preoccupied with my work and climbing up the corporate ladder that a spiritual life didn't even enter my mind!

So, I guess you could call me a bonafide skeptic who was pretty smug and pretty happy in my life, although, in my heart of hearts, I longed for more meaning.

At the end of this trip to LA, I had some spare time before having to head for the airport. Knowing I love books, a friend of mine suggested I check out The Bodhi Tree Book Store. The Bodhi Tree is a sacred symbol in Buddhism - it is the place where Buddha attained enlightenment after meditating for 49 days.

Of course, I didn't even realize it was a spiritual bookstore before I got there. As I was browsing around, a book fell off a shelf onto my head. I kid you not! The book was Louise Hay's *You Can Heal Your Life*, a wonderful eye-opener for a novice. Of course, with such an unlikely intro, I simply had to buy it immediately.

In retrospect and knowing what I know now that book falling on my head was no accident but what I consider a "God thing" …a divine intervention giving me a tap on the shoulder to ignite my interest in the bigger picture than the narrow world I was living in.

During my flight home to Boston, I devoured the entire Louise Hay book. At times, it rang so true, I found myself crying. Reading *You Can Heal Your Life* was a life-changing event for me and provided the divine spark needed for me to embark on a spiritual journey. From that point on, I went from being a spiritual skeptic to an enthusiastic seeker.

I am something of a closet bookworm and love to learn through the written word. After I read Louise Hay's book, I gobbled up everything I could get my hands on that was spiritual…*A Course in Miracles*, Marianne Williamson, Jerry Jampolsky, Wayne Dyer, Ernest Holmes, Deepak Chopra, Carolyn Myss, Paul Ferrini, Alan Cohen, David Hawkins, Gina Lake, and Eckart Tolle, to name a few. So, in this book, I am not giving you only my own thoughts; I draw from many thought leaders in the field.

You're about to embark on a journey that you'll never turn back from. I don't believe you have picked up this book by accident. You're either ready to launch into a spiritual life or to enhance the one you have. I feel privileged to be taking this journey with you. I hope I can make a difference to you in your life as well as for everyone else who picks up this book. I wrote *A Spiritual Tool Kit* because I wish I could have had access to a primer or 'how to" book to guide me at the start of my spiritual path.

Thank you for sharing your journey with me and for spending some of your limited time reading one spiritual junkie's experiences and perspective.

It takes time, dedication, and commitment to nurture an inner life and to follow a spiritual path…but well worth the effort. If you've been wondering how you could possibly fulfill the demands of a spiritual life yet keep up with the responsibilities and social commitments of everyday life, read on. Spiritual writer and teacher, Jack Kornfield, has a terrific, tongue-in-cheek title to one of his books, *After the Ecstasy, the Laundry*. So don't worry…everyone has this same concern. Please know that, once you get started, the time and work you must dedicate will be less daunting and well worth the effort to gain peace of mind, clarity, and more happiness.

The purpose of this book is to give you the tools to become more deeply connected to Spirit, to God, to the Divine, and to the wisdom of the Universe. It is designed to be a no-nonsense, simple intro or refresher to spirituality and to present a clear path to a more heartfelt connection in daily living.

Some of us are religious, others are spiritual, while still others are just curious. It doesn't make a difference – whatever soothes your soul and puts you in touch with the Divine is fine by me AND I'm sure by God as well!

Most of us already have a profound belief in the sacredness of life and the innate wisdom of Nature. Here are the goals this book has been created to accomplish:

- Bring your life into a place of harmony and balance

- Feel good about yourself

- Change your thinking; change your life

- Open yourself to new ideas and fresh ways of doing things

- Learn to interpret events and circumstances optimistically

- Listen to your intuition

- Use proven tools to strengthen your spiritual practice

- Enjoy well-being and positive relationships

- Experience peace and fulfillment

- Become a ray of light to the people around you

Some of the topics covered in this book are affirmations, prayer, meditation, gratitude, forgiveness, intuition, self-love, kindness, and empathy. There will also be some new concepts I'll be introducing to you, such as "The Cosmic Coincidence Control Center" and "Aha! Moments." Suggested spiritual literature and music appear at the end of the book. I even provide you with my personal playlists that I hope you'll enjoy.

Each chapter will finish with some of my own personal experiences that illustrate how that chapter's topic is applied in real life. You might be surprised how willing I am to share things about myself (not all pretty!) that most people wouldn't think of revealing.

Trust me, being spiritually oriented doesn't result, at least in my case, in a trouble-free life or instant Nirvana. I still have plenty of shortcomings and a slew of foibles that haven't magically disappeared. But I haven't lost my sense of humor (put me against a wall and shoot me if that ever happens!!), and my love for people has grown exponentially over the years. While I find myself to be just another "Bozo on the Bus of Life", my spiritual learnings and practices have resulted in my being calmer, more positive, kinder, more creative, infinitely happier and much of the time at peace.

Regardless of what your day job may be, your real work is to raise your own vibrational level so that you can help those around you to raise theirs and, ultimately, to assist the whole planet to resonate to a higher vibration of love. We do this by cultivating a spiritual life and "walking the walk" with dedication, practice, and humor.

Don't let your experience in spiritual learning be dry and boring…remember that joy and happiness are ultimate goals, so be sure to laugh at yourself AND me as you go through this book.

If you are drawn to strengthening your spiritual connection and would like to build upon the sacred aspects of your life, this book can help you enhance what you are already doing or, if you are a newcomer, provide you with some structure and basics for getting started.

Thank you for reading! Let's begin.

Much love,

Kathleen

YOU'RE A SPIRITUAL BEING

You're Not Just a Body

Surprise! Who would've thought it? You're not just a body; you're a spirit as well. Philosopher and teacher Pierre Teilhard de Chardin once wrote:

"We are not human beings having a spiritual

experience. We are spiritual beings

having a human experience."

There was a time when I would've dismissed that as a bunch of malarkey—or, at best, completely irrelevant. But now? Those words ring true for me, and I stand by them. It takes a leap of faith to view ourselves this way, but once you do, it's as clear and undeniable as the nose on your face: this is the truth.

Another way I like to think of it is that every person on the planet carries a spark of the Divine, a small piece of the Universal Force within. While we may act like we're limited and temporary, we're anything but. And maybe, just maybe, it's time we begin appreciating this life, and its lessons, as something profoundly sacred.

Astrophysicist Neil deGrasse Tyson once said:

"Not only are we in the universe, but the universe

is also in us. I don't know of any deeper

spiritual feeling than what that

brings upon me."

Of course, leave it to Woody Allen to say:

"I'm astounded by people who want to know the

Universe when it's hard enough to find

your way around Chinatown."

And from Lily Tomlin:

"Did you know, in the entire Universe, we are

the only intelligent life forms thought to

have a Miss Universe contest?"

So seriously, what does it mean to be a "spiritual being?" In plain terms, I believe it means we're connected to something greater than ourselves. We are far more than our physical bodies or our everyday lives. Being human is temporary, but our essence is eternal and infinite.

As Marianne Williamson puts it:

"I wasn't just randomly thrown

onto a sea of rocks."

Nancy Colier writes in *Psychology Today*:

> *"We are more than just the sum total of our thoughts,*
>
> *our feelings, and our life situation that we are living*
>
> *in the moment. We have a sense of being larger*
>
> *or more infinite than just our little 'me'."*

It might seem like we're born into this world as a completely blank Etch A Sketch. But I believe that, as eternal beings, our journey through time is far more complex than that. Exactly how does it all work? I have no idea! Our eyes, miraculous as they are, can only see about 1% of the visible light spectrum. So, the idea that we could grasp the full scope of reality through these very human set of eyes feels, well... a bit absurd.

Anthon St. Maarten wrote:

> *"You are only one thing. You are a Divine Being. An all-powerful Creator.*
>
> *You are a Deity in jeans and a t-shirt, and within you dwells the*
>
> *infinite wisdom of the ages and the sacred creative force*
>
> *of All that is, will be, and ever was."*

Recently, I came across a list of twelve signs that indicate you're awakening spiritually. Personally, I'm trying to hone my skills in all of them...not an easy task!

Spiritual Growth: 12 Signs You're Growing and Evolving

(Compiled by Aletheia in *Lone Wolf Magazine*)

1. You embrace challenges as lessons and opportunities.

2. You see through the seduction of the material world.

3. Your sensitivity has heightened.

4. You feel more love and compassion for yourself, others, and the world.

5. You stop seeing life in black-or-white, dualistic thinking.

6. You show more understanding toward difficult people.

7. You recognize that life is cyclical and spiral-like.

8. You become less attached to your mental stories.

9. You find it easier to slow down and do nothing.

10. You are more interested in letting go of the old than gaining the new.

11. You develop a greater capacity for discernment.

12. You begin to experience more moments of "ordinary magic."

I do know this for sure…because of my spiritual studies and personal experiences as I've traversed this planet, I have absolute faith in a Divine Presence I can count on. I know for sure my soul is on an eternal journey.

It's kind of like going through life's ups and downs with a spiritual superhero starter-pack that always supports you: Batman's Batmobile, Popeye's spinach, and Superman's phone booth, rolled into one. Not a bad combo.

A Transcendental Experience

I've had a few transcendent moments in my life—those rare flashes where I believe we get a brief glimpse of true reality. One such moment happened when I was living in Boston and riding the T (that's what they call their subway or metro system). At certain points, the T rises above ground, running parallel with the traffic. I was on the Green Line on a beautiful spring day, heading downtown.

Just before the train entered a dark tunnel, I "saw" something—not with my physical eyes exactly, but with some deeper sense. For a split second, I perceived how deeply connected we all were on that bright, sunlit train. I recognized the divinity in that small group. It's hard to describe, but I was suddenly filled with immense respect for each and every one of those souls around me (including myself)—all of us patiently slogging through life, bouncing around on the same subway as Divine beings.

It was almost funny, in a cosmic kind of way. But mostly, it left me with a deep, momentary reverence: a clear awareness that everyone I encounter carries the eternal spark of God within them. It was an overwhelming sense of "we're all in this together."—I experienced a moment of pure reverence for life.

A Course in Miracles (ACIM) is a spiritual path that I utilize and hold dear. It is a self-study program of spiritual guidance that helps you view life with a unique lens as you integrate its daily lessons into your life. As students of ACIM, we are encouraged to view every encounter, whether with close friends, total strangers, longtime companions, or fleeting passersby as a Holy Encounter. Trust me, if you truly try to live by this idea, you'll be amazed by how your mindset shifts. Kindness, respect, gratitude and compassion become your default settings. Not because you're trying to be good, but because you suddenly see who people really are.

Feeling the Presence of My Mother

How many people do you know who've felt a message or a presence from a loved one who has passed? I would guess many, although some are reluctant to share these types of experiences, but if you ask them, they will tell a compelling story. These kinds of moments, whether in dreams, a sudden knowing, or an unexplainable sign, can be unsettling, but also so welcome.

I was especially close to my mother, and believe I received two clear signs from her after she passed away at age 69.

I simply love Christmas…most likely because my parents always made it such a special season. Among my many holiday decorations was a treasured Nutcracker that doubles as a music box. I had given it to my mother years earlier, and it always reminds me of her.

One night, as I was heading to bed, the Nutcracker suddenly started playing the kids' song, "Toyland." I hadn't touched it since placing it on the table. I *knew* in my gut—it was her. It was her way of letting me know she was there with me, with our family, sharing in the spirit of the holiday. What a comforting and magical feeling it was!

My Mother's Inimitable Sense of Humor

The second time I felt my mother sending me a message was equally powerful. Many years after her death, I was walking home from work in Washington, D.C., missing her deeply. I started feeling sorry for myself, lamenting the fact that I had lost both my parents so young. (My father passed away at just 47.) I even found myself feeling envious of friends who still had their parents and bemoaning my fate, thinking, "Why did I have to become an orphan so early in life?"

Then I opened my front door and found a copy of *Time* magazine on the floor that had been put through the mail slot. The cover story that was looking up at me? It was about the many people my age or older, struggling to care for their aging parents. Suddenly, I paused. In that moment, I realized I was, in a strange way, lucky. I'd already been through the loss of my parents, so I didn't have to face the drawn-out suffering and caretaking challenges so many others did. I *knew* my mother was guiding my perspective, offering even a little Irish gallows humor, just when I needed it most.

A Visitation from a Beloved Friend Who Had Passed

Another deeply moving experience involved my dearest friend, Julie. She was my Soul Sister, wise, loving, and spiritually radiant. We talked every day; she was one of the most enlightened people I've ever known. Her faith and presence were constant sources of inspiration for me.

Julie passed away at the age of 59 after a long battle with uterine cancer. On her last day in the hospital, she developed sepsis. Along with her family, I was by her side holding her hand when she died. One of the fears I carried was that she might suffer something horrific in her final days. A friend had once told me about a woman who developed sepsis in the hospital and ended up losing both her hands and feet. That image haunted me. So, I prayed that Julie would die rather than suffer such a fate.

After she died, I was in terrible grief. New Year's was approaching, and I chose to skip the annual dinner party and celebration I usually attended. But on New Year's Eve, suddenly I intuitively knew I should just stop by for a quick drink. When I arrived and greeted someone at the party, I nearly fainted. She reached out to introduce herself to me with a handshake, and I saw that she had a prosthetic device on her right hand. Then I saw that she was missing her other hand *and* both feet.

What are the odds of this happening randomly? I believe that Julie was trying to communicate to me that I was praying for the right thing. She was letting me know this was a condition she didn't want to suffer through and that she appreciated my prayers to spare her.

What are your amazing stories? I'd love to hear them. Write me at kathleenpasley@hotmail.com, if the spirit moves you.

RELATIONSHIPS

How to Improve Them

As an inveterate "people person" and enthusiastic networker, it's no surprise that relationships are the most important part of my life. Come to think of it, relationships are the most important part of everyone's life!

We all have a deep need for love—both to give it and to receive it—so it makes sense that relationships sit at the center of both our worldly and spiritual lives.

At their best, relationships overflow with love, support, and meaning. But they can also be the most challenging aspect of life, fraught with misunderstandings, emotional turmoil, and even hatred. As the old saying goes:

"Most couples haven't had hundreds of arguments;

they've had the same argument

hundreds of times!"

When I speak of relationships, I mean all kinds, not just romantic partnerships. That includes friendships, work relationships, family dynamics, and most importantly, the relationship we have with ourselves. Relationships come in all shapes and sizes, from brief encounters to lifelong commitments. And each one, no matter how fleeting or frustrating, carries spiritual meaning and purpose. They help us grow, whether we like it or not.

Not that we always like what that growth entails. It's been said:

"God doesn't give you the people you want,

He gives you the people you need."

To help you, to hurt you, to challenge you, to leave you, to love you… and to make you the person you were meant to be.

But the truth is, relationships come in all sizes and shapes – from the most casual to the most meaningful.

Family Relationships

You might look at this the same way George Burns did:

Happiness is having a large, loving, caring,

close-knit family in another city.

Relationships with Friends

Could be you experience them this way:

Best friends don't care if your house is clean.

They care if you have some wine.

Relationships with Colleagues

For me the internal dialogue can go something like this:

I will not kill my co-workers.

I will not kill my co-workers.

I will not...

OK. maybe just one.

    A Course in Miracles makes it clear that no encounter is accidental. I find it helpful to trust that God places the right people into my life at the right time for the right reason—and often, I don't have a clue what that reason is!

    The truth is, you are both a student and a teacher. Not only that, every other human being on the planet plays these two roles as well. You'll find that when you teach something to others, that's when you really learn it. I know this from experience. I've been a teacher (not always a good one!); even more times, I've been a student. Believe me, I have lots to learn. And if there's one thing I've discovered about spiritual lessons…you can't rush or force the process. You just have to stay open and let life unfold.

    Every encounter we have is a teaching and learning opportunity. The Divine Spirit has a way of bringing the exact people we need into our lives to deliver the precise lesson we need at that moment.

The question is: Are we paying enough attention to learn the lesson? I know for myself, I'm a great multitasker: I can listen, ignore, and forget all at the same time!

Deepak Chopra says:

> *"There are no accidents… There is only one purpose*
>
> *that we haven't yet understood."*

Karen Casey writes:

> *"No one is without purpose in our journey. No one."*

I could always buy that meeting a partner or spouse could easily have a bit of the "grand design" in it. Maybe the same goes for your parents, your children, your best friend, your favorite professor, a key mentor, or a spiritual guide—those major relationships that help define or direct your life.

But what about your interactions with the garbage man? The teller at your bank? The "space cadet" who rear-ends your car? Your neighbor, the woman sitting next to you on a plane, the members of your book group, the kid who runs into you on his bike, or the person who walks by without returning your smile? They are ALL important.

Spiritual teacher Doreen Virtue writes:

> *"Every relationship has a spiritual purpose that helps us grow*
>
> *better and stronger. Sometimes our most challenging*
>
> *relationships bring the greatest personal blessings.*
>
> *From them, we learn about forgiveness,*

patience, and other virtues."

According to *A Course in Miracles (ACIM)*, there are three levels of teaching and learning that are always at work in our lives. The first level is what we think of as a casual encounter. The second level is a more sustained relationship in which, for a time, two people enter into a fairly intense teaching–learning situation and then appear to separate. The third level is a relationship that, once formed, lasts a lifetime.

At this level, *ACIM* says.

> *"Each person is given a chosen learning partner who presents*
>
> *him with unlimited opportunities for learning."*

As mentioned before, we're encouraged to consider every interaction with another human being as a Holy Encounter—one centered in peace, love, and respect.

During major disagreements in any kind of relationship, being open to a shift in your perception—or asking the Universe for another way to see the situation—can be invaluable. Every once in a while, that shift comes effortlessly. I consider those moments to be miracles... magical gifts from God. I'll talk about that more later.

A Relationship Can Be Healed in a Nanosecond

I was working with the owner of a graphic design company, who I was also dating (yes, I know... jumbo mistake right off the bat!) I had hired Keith to design and print a newly conceived and full colored newsletter that had to be ready by a specific date so it could be introduced to the Board.

When the finished job arrived, I was furious. The paper was flimsy; the color quality was horrible, and the whole thing looked completely second-rate. I had trusted him, and it was clear he'd cut corners in every way possible to increase his profits at my expense. I was enraged.

It was already late in the day, just about 15 hours before the Board meeting where the newsletter was going to be unveiled. I stormed over to Keith's office, spitting bullets. I launched into a full-on tirade, wagging my finger and ranting about how he had delivered shoddy work and left me in an impossible position.

But then, mid-rant, something stopped me. I was suddenly overwhelmed by a deep sense of love for this person, not necessarily in a romantic way, but as a fellow human being. And I could feel his love for me in return.

The moment my mind shifted, I went from rage to compassion and could only think of hugging him. And in that same moment, he dropped his defenses and simply said: "Let's fix this."

Together, we spent the entire night, until 6 am, working to have a new print run completed. We returned to my office just in time to place the beautiful newsletters into the Board packets before the meeting began.

As I'm telling this story now, I realize this experience may sound like no big deal or particularly out of the ordinary. After all, we've all had a zillion fights and made up close to a zillion times! But this experience was different. The internal shift in my perception of the situation was so dramatic, I felt it was so sudden, involuntary, and complete that it could only have come through the Grace of God. It was as though extreme hate had shifted to complete love and compassion in a nanosecond. I have never forgotten the experience. It truly felt like a miracle.

Rumi wrote:

"Be a lamp, or a lifeboat, or a ladder. Help someone's

soul heal. Walk out of your house

like a shepherd."

That day, I experienced what it means to be both the lamp and the ladder.

You'll Never Know How You Might Make a Difference

There was a time when I became a teacher to someone without even realizing it. In fact, I had absolutely no recollection of even knowing her, let alone saying something that might change the course of her life! Here's how the story goes:

Many years ago, I met Edemir Rossi, a powerful spiritual healer, intuitive and teacher who works on people energetically. When he works with someone, Edemir first talks to the individual in a kind of therapy session on steroids! His intuitive gift allows him to focus on the person's issues quickly and in depth. Then the person lies on a massage table while Edemir works on him or her energetically.

I believed so much in Edemir's ability to help people, I invited him to work out of a spare bedroom in my house in Washington, DC. A short two-week visit eventually turned into his coming to the States from Brazil for six months a year and this schedule continued for 17 years.

Edemir helps clients with a myriad of problems – physical, emotional, spiritual and relationship-related. I invariably met lots of the people he worked with and in many cases got to know them. Since Edemir worked a nine-hour day, I met more people than I could possibly remember. Many of them came through my door distraught, seeking his help.

One of them was a woman named Donna. I don't remember meeting her at all, but she later reminded me that we were sitting in my living room, and she told me why she wanted to see Edemir. She was trying to have a baby, but it wasn't happening. I could see she was in a really distressed emotional state, so after her session, I suggested we take a walk.

Apparently (and I swear, I don't recall a single second of this!), we spent the next hour walking around Georgetown. During that time, she opened up more about her relationship with her boyfriend, and I told her, quite bluntly, that he sounded like a real jerk who had worked hard at damaging her self-esteem. I suggested she give up the idea of marrying him and that having his baby could be a complete disaster. I also told her how remarkable she was since she was so clearly lacking in confidence. I told her she deserved so much more than that boyfriend could ever give her.

And remember—this was to a complete stranger! I still don't know what came over me that day. Divine download? Cosmic boldness? Who knows!

Fast forward ten years. Out of the blue, I received a heartfelt thank you email from Donna. She told me she had never forgotten my kindness or that message I gave her on that long walk. She said it changed her life.

She ended up leaving that boyfriend, marrying a truly wonderful husband, and having two beautiful daughters. To this day, I remain completely flabbergasted, both by my cheekiness and by the fact that I have no memory of an encounter that ended up being so life-shaping for someone.

But here's the real kicker…the advice I gave Donna about her boyfriend? It was the exact same advice I should have been giving myself about the man I was in love with at the time! I desperately needed to learn what I was teaching that day, but it took an excruciatingly long time to apply that advice to myself! I could see the truth when it came to someone else's situation, but I couldn't apply it to my own life. Talk about a teaching/learning moment. In this case, I did a good job teaching, but I was a *very* slow learner!

Avoid Judging People You Don't Know

I was having a birthday celebration dinner with a best friend at a super expensive, trendy Indian restaurant in Washington, D.C. Seated next to us was a couple who, by appearances, didn't seem particularly well-dressed or worldly. They didn't look especially sophisticated—or to be honest, very sharp.

They lingered over the menu, clearly having a hard time deciding what to order. I leaned over to my friend and whispered, "I bet those two have never been to an Indian restaurant before." My friend, not missing a beat, added, "I bet they've never been to the city before!"

Not long after our little snark fest, I turned to the woman beside me and asked—rather condescendingly, "Did you figure out what to order yet?"

She smiled and responded, "Oh, we come here at least once a week! We just have a hard time choosing because we love everything on the menu. Honestly, it's better than anything we had in India."

Cut to our jaws hitting the table. Turns out, they were far from the "duds" we had so smugly assumed they were. She was a college professor, and he held a prestigious government position. Oops!

It may seem like a brief, silly moment, but that couple turned out to be important teachers for me. What did I learn? I tend to make condescending snap judgments about people I don't even know.

I must admit, I still find that I judge way too much. But since that "minor league" encounter, I've improved. Or at the very least, I catch myself in the middle of those condemning thoughts, which is a step in the right direction.

SELF-LOVE

Needed Before You Can Love Someone Else

Wouldn't it be wonderful if believing we are lovable was a constant in our lives? As much as I've grown in this area, I'm still amazed at how quickly I can slip back into the grip of negative self-talk.

Some days, believing I'm lovable feels easy, natural, even. At other times, it seems impossible! When I'm on top of the world, it's an easy one. Like when I've accomplished something meaningful, when I think I look good, when someone tells me they love me, when I've helped someone, or when someone laughs at my jokes. Really, any kind of positive feedback will do!

But then, there are the other days when I can feel totally unlovable if someone criticizes me, when I make a mistake, when I do something stupid, when I don't like the way I look in the mirror, when I feel rejected, misunderstood, disrespected—or when I catch myself thinking I'm getting old. The list goes on and on.

That fear of not being enough or of being unworthy is something most of us deal with—not constantly, but for many of us, too often. Whether we're aware of it or not, I believe we all carry a deep longing to feel: "I'm loved… no matter what. I'm accepted for who I am, warts and all."

There are times when I find it hard to believe either of these are true. It's such a gift when someone we love affirms them for us. But giving that same kind of love and acceptance to ourselves? That's the real challenge.

When I feel good about myself, it kind of goes like this:

OK. I'M HERE.

So what are your other two wishes?

I am also pretty good at adhering to the principle that:

If you're searching for the one person

that will change your life,

take a look in the mirror.

I actually like people who speak "fluent sarcasm" and love jokes about the absurdity of self-absorption or narcissism, not to mention life in general. As in:

I hate it when I go to hug someone

really sexy and my face smashes right

into the mirror.

or

Think I am sarcastic? Watch me

pretend to care.

or

If you don't want to come to my house

because I burn sage that means

the sage is working.

And even when others do offer us that kind of unconditional support, it can vanish in a flash if we make a big blooper (which can be quite often as we stumble through life as mere mortals). This is especially true if that mistake affects them. That blanket of love can evaporate in quick order.

Louise Hay, in her writing and teaching, referred to this pattern as the "Myth of Inadequacy." The thoughts that swirl around in our heads might sound like:

I'm not successful enough.

I'm not talented enough.

I haven't done enough with my life.

I'm not good enough and never will be.

I always screw up my relationships.

I haven't lived up to my potential.

I really blew that one.

And on... and on...

But God sees us completely differently. To Him, we are always the "cat's meow"; the "bee's knees"; and "peachy keen." All around sensational. Out of this world. That's how He sees our spirit—our true self—beneath all the "gunk" of human imperfection. In God's eyes, you are lovable. Always.

This God doesn't dwell on judgment, criticism, or comparison. His message is always simple, direct, and unconditional: "I love you, regardless of your mistakes, kid."

Louise Hay asserts that the most important thing you can do in this life is to love and accept yourself. Think of it this way: while we all set so many goals for ourselves—career, health, relationships—what if our real job, our fundamental purpose, is deep self-acceptance and self-love? Now that's not only surprising news... it can be a very tall order.

Brené Brown puts it this way:

"True acceptance comes from understanding that

we are all flawed and making peace with both

ourselves and others."

One of my very favorite affirmations that I try to say in the mirror to myself every morning is: *"I love and accept myself exactly as I am."*

Louise Hay wrote:

"Love is a deep appreciation for who we are. We accept all the different parts of

ourselves—our little peculiarities, the embarrassments, the things we

may not do so well, and all the wonderful qualities as well. We

accept the whole package with love. Unconditionally."

And the eternally-wise Mr. Rogers once said:

"You don't ever have to do anything sensational

for people to love you."

Well, how about that? Being lovable without having to qualify for it?? The irony is most of us believe this to be true for others; we love our friends and family despite their flaws. But when it comes to us, we often have this nasty habit of thinking we have to constantly prove ourselves to justify our existence!

Some say the only way to improve is to be self-critical—to assess ourselves harshly, to be brutally honest. I disagree. I believe we are all works in progress and masterpieces at the same time. So yes, work on yourself—just don't berate yourself while doing it.

A Course in Miracles teaches that in order to truly see ourselves—and others—we must ask for help from the spirit world. We must be willing to shift our perception and see from a higher vantage point. And from that perspective, the truth is always the same: YOU ARE LOVED.

We must remember:

> *We are braver than we believe,*
>
> *Stronger than we seem, and*
>
> *Smarter than we think.*
>
> *Life is tough, but we are tougher.*

Embarrassing Moments in Corporate Life

When I worked in the corporate world, I frequently gave speeches, presentations, and workshops to both large and small groups. One time, I was scheduled to speak at a marketing conference in San Francisco, hosted by the largest marketing consulting firm in the insurance industry. My workshop, set for the first afternoon, was entitled "Getting Your Customers to Love You."

Now, let's face it—insurance agents aren't exactly the most beloved people in the world.

As Woody Allen said in one of his movies:

"There are worse things than death. Like

spending an evening with an

insurance salesman!"

My goal was to encourage the audience to write correspondence and marketing materials that didn't sound so stiff, cold, or full of legalese. In other words, urging them to sound more conversational and like a real person.

On the morning of my talk, all attendees gathered for a plenary session. The speaker was a high-powered attorney, and his topic was negotiation. He gave a powerful talk on how tough you need to be to get what you want, how you must be willing to walk away if you want leverage. His message was bold, assertive, and very effective. Of course, he had the demeanor to match—a classic tough guy, encouraging the audience to adopt the same no-nonsense attitude.

I was sinking into my chair. How was I supposed to follow that with a talk about getting your customers to love you? Suddenly, my presentation felt lightweight and sappy in comparison to his hard-hitting message. But I had no choice—I went ahead with my presentation and delivered the talk. The turnout for my breakout session was not that large (golf time, you know) but even so, I was mortified. Why would anyone want to hear me after the morning's hard-hitting keynote? I soldiered on but felt less than pleased with my performance and was completely deflated by the end of the day.

That evening, a reception was planned at Mondavi Winery in Napa Valley—a welcome break, I thought, after a rough, rather humiliating day. I asked one of the conference organizers what the dress code was. She told me it was business casual.

So, I dressed accordingly—slacks, a green blazer, and a casual blouse (how could I ever forget my outfit)?! But the moment I got on the bus, I realized every other woman was in cocktail attire. Cocktail dresses, heels, upswept hairdos, the whole nine yards. Once again, I nearly died with mortification and seriously considered stumbling off the bus and bailing out on going to the winery.

But I told myself: This is the social highlight of the conference, and part of your work here is to connect with people. Just suck it up and go.

During the ride, I kept repeating in my head: "Get over yourself! Do you think Mother Teresa—one of your idols—would give this a second thought?"

Of course, I'm hardly Mother Teresa and just couldn't take a cavalier attitude towards my blunder. Still, I gingerly got off the bus, walked into the winery, grabbed a glass of wine, and skulked to a quiet spot away from the crowd.

And then…something amazing happened. An insurance agent from Canada approached me and said how much he loved my workshop. He told me it was such a refreshing contrast to "that pompous jerk who spoke in the morning." I could not believe it!

To top it off, on the bus ride back to the hotel, I sat next to a young man who told me how much he admired me and thought my presence and message were so uplifting after that intense morning session.

So many lessons came out of that experience. I wasn't so bad after all. My message had landed with the right people who needed it. And neither my outfit nor my topic was the point. All was well.

You Can't Please All the People All of the Time

As part of my work as a marketing professional, I occasionally took on clients outside of my company on a freelance basis. One of those clients was a high-end health club located inside a fancy hotel in Cambridge, Massachusetts, just across the Salt and Pepper Bridge that goes over the Charles River from Boston.

At the time, I lived on Beacon Hill and didn't own a car. Parking was such a hassle (not to mention, crazily expensive!), and digging out when there was a snowstorm was brutal. Boston is a very walkable city, so being without a car was a real blessing. Thankfully, I could hop on the T and get to the hotel in just a few stops.

I really liked the manager and ended up doing several projects to help bring more members into the club. In exchange, I received generous compensation and a complimentary membership at the club, which, let me tell you, was a nice perk.

My strategy was to use direct mail. I focused on creating attractive and eye-catching designs with compelling messaging that would stand out for people in the surrounding area. Each mailer was hand-addressed and stamped with a commemorative stamp to make it feel more personal, and less like junk mail. My approach was always to try to "cut through the clutter" of traditional direct mail.

The results were phenomenal. With every mailing, we far surpassed our membership goal. Since the club was quite expensive, we often included a $500 discount on the initiation fee, valid if someone joined before a specific date the following month.

But then, one day, I was shocked and disturbed when I received a scathing personal letter in the mail. A woman—who, based on her tone, must have been having a very bad day—was furious. The envelope she'd received had confetti and balloon images on the front, and she assumed it was an invitation to a party. When she opened it and discovered it was a health club promotion, she ripped it up in outrage and took the time to tell me all about it.

I was honestly shocked—and more than a little upset. Here I had put time, care, and creativity into this campaign, and someone had not only rejected it but felt the need to lash out about it.

I vented to a friend who listened patiently and then asked, "How many pieces did you send out?"

"Three thousand???, I replied. She rolled her eyes and said, "And you got one complaint? Seriously? You can't get everyone to love you. Get over it."

And... she was right. So, I did.

Comments from "The Peanut Gallery"

As I've mentioned, I often gave workshops for relatively small groups, and most attendees seemed happy with my presentations. But one day, while I was speaking in the Midwest, a man came up to me during the break and said, "Kathy, I'd really appreciate it if you didn't use God—our Lord's name, in vain."

I was stunned. I hadn't been aware of saying anything that might have offended him, and I certainly didn't realize I was using "God" so often in a casual way. I was completely taken aback and, truthfully, more than a little annoyed.

It was one of those moments where I had to make a conscious choice: either let someone else's opinion derail me or release it and move forward. These were costly lessons for me in the beginning, because I used to be far too thin-skinned to handle criticism. Just one negative comment could throw me off for days.

But with time and a few more humbling experiences, I learned to toughen up and stay grounded in my own truth. Now, at the end of the day, I know this: I am lovable and capable, regardless of comments from The Peanut Gallery!

Love Yourself... But Don't Take Yourself Too Seriously

One year, I was staying at a friend's apartment in New York City during the Christmas Holiday. We had tickets to go to the Vienna Boys Choir at Carnegie Hall, and I was so looking forward to it.

Before we left, my hair was kind of a mess, so I asked Carol if I could borrow her hairspray to see if I could improve on my "look." I almost never use hairspray, but this was a night when I sprayed on a powerful dose for good measure. When I looked at the spray container, I realized I had just sprayed my hair with Secret deodorant!

While I was complaining to my friend and myself about my stupidity (plus laughing at the absurdity of it all!), I decided the heck with it…I really wanted to see the concert, and who was going to notice anyway? So, I went out with a halo of smelly deodorant around my head.

But in my heart of hearts, I was worried that people would notice an unusual odor coming from me. If my friend had been a date, I probably would have hidden in the bathroom. Well, I needn't have worried because guess what happened?

Before we went to the theater, we had a drink at the Russian Tea Room, right next door to Carnegie Hall – a great experience if you've never been. I've always loved the place! We were sitting at the bar enjoying our glass of wine when a man came up to me and said, "What is that wonderful perfume you are wearing? I rarely compliment women on their scent, but that perfume on you is fantastic."

Could be that the clue to loving myself at ALL times is in a spray can – my very own SECRET to being loved unconditionally!

THE COSMIC COINCIDENCE
CONTROL CENTER

No Encounters Are Random

How do we manage to meet certain people? Why do some events happen so unexpectedly? We all have stories, those moments when, by the slimmest thread of coincidence, we avoided a disaster or stumbled upon a life-changing experience. Maybe it was a chance meeting with someone who would later become important in our lives. I choose to think of these moments as gifts from a knowing, loving Universe, and believe that my life is being divinely guided by intelligent action.

The first time I heard about the *Cosmic Coincidence Control Center*, it immediately made sense to me. In the past, I used to think every encounter with another human being was random. But over time, I've come to believe that it's not so simple, that the *Cosmic Coincidence Control Center* is quietly at work in all our lives.

Skeptics might say something like this:

PERFECT has seven letters and so does

MEEEEEE. Coincidence?

I think not.

or

Dinosaurs didn't bowl and now

they are extinct. Coincidence?

Think about your own life, your experiences, and the people you've met. Isn't it easy to imagine the Universe working behind the scenes, gently shaping your path? You might even picture a committee of otherworldly beings moving the chess pieces of your life, aligning events so that you cross paths with exactly the right people at the right time.

Another reason we connect with certain people, I believe, is that our thoughts and level of consciousness are often aligned. Alan Cohen, in *A Daily Dose of Sanity*, suggests that we naturally attract people, romantic partners, co-workers, and friends who match our beliefs, values, interests, and habits of thought. Like calls to like. Your mind becomes a magnet for those on a similar frequency.

Carl Jung, who believed in a unifying consciousness behind the Universe, encouraged us to pay attention to these moments of synchronicity. He said,

"Synchronicity is an ever-present reality for those

who have eyes to see.

As someone wisely said, there are no coincidences—only divine appointments.

Nancy Thayer put it this way:

"The Universe is always speaking to us… Sending us little messages, causing coincidences and serendipities. Reminding us to stop, to look around, and to believe in something else, something more."

A Meeting on a Bus (of all things!)

I once visited one of my brothers in New Jersey for my birthday before heading into New York City for more celebrating. I came within a hair's breadth of missing the bus to Manhattan. It was freezing, snow on the ground, wind whipping, and we were running so late that my brother had to slam on the brakes and stop his car in front of the departing bus just to get me on.

The scowling bus driver helped me with my bags and barked at me to find a seat—and fast. Normally, I avoid sitting next to strangers on planes, trains, or buses. But in this case, I could feel the hostile vibes from the other passengers, mirroring the driver's irritation at our delayed departure. So, I quickly and sheepishly took the first available seat, next to a man who turned out to be both attractive and fascinating.

We chatted nonstop the whole way into the city (really, only a 30-minute ride!) and sparked up a friendship that has lasted to this day. Fast forward: that man, Igor, became a fabulous friend and fellow spiritual seeker. After eleven years, he's still one of the dearest people in my life and we have become spiritual partners.

Connecting with a Brazilian Healer Who Changed My Life

Back in the 1990s, I attended a four-day workshop with Barbara Brennan, author of *Hands of Light*. There were 250 students in the room. On the first day, I sat next to a woman but instantly felt uncomfortable, with a strong inner nudge to move. I almost never do that, but I didn't want to spend the entire session feeling "off." So, hoping not to insult her, I quietly moved seats (which I never, ever do) and found myself next to the Brazilian healer, Edemir, who I've mentioned before.

Here's the wild part: Edemir had done the exact same thing. He'd moved seats, in his case, worried that where he was sitting would make it hard to follow the leader's English. And somehow, the two of us ended up sitting side by side.

Edemir changed my life in many ways. After September 11th I reconnected with him by calling him in Brazil to see if he would come to help my many friends (myself included!) who were all traumatized. His first visit lasted two weeks, and it grew exponentially from there.

Edemir eventually came to Washington, DC for at least six months out of the year. He worked out of my home for seventeen years, often for nine hours a day, offering powerful healing sessions to countless people. I handled all his public relations, marketing, and scheduling - sharing who he was and why people should come to him as well as tracking and balancing his busy days. Together, we also led and managed dozens of seminars, workshops, and retreats in the United States and sacred places across the world, such as Brazil, India, Mexico, Peru, and Guatemala. (I did all of this while still working at my real day job as a fundraiser.) I was so committed to Edemir's healing gift and the impact he had on so many, this work became my avocation for many years.

As Barbara Dillingham once said:

"Life is not a path of coincidence, happenstance, and luck, but rather an unexplainable, meticulously charted course for one to touch the lives

of others and make a difference in the world."

My experience with Edemir certainly taught me just how true that is.

A Life Changing Miracle on a Train

My brother Peter had hoped to become a doctor since the fourth grade. He was born for the job! But after one poor college chemistry grade, getting into medical school became a real problem. Feeling discouraged, he boarded a train from Boston to New York, unsure of his future.

Ready to give up on his dream, he was feeling depressed and hopeless. By chance or cosmic design, he ended up sitting next to a young doctor from Ireland. After hearing Peter's story, the doctor suggested he apply to the prestigious Royal College of Surgeons in Dublin. This stranger thought there was a good chance Peter could be accepted, especially since he was second-generation Irish.

Lo and behold, Peter applied to the school and was accepted. He did exceptionally well, and after two years, transferred back to the U.S., eventually becoming Chief Resident at a top New York City hospital before launching his practice as an internist. He's gone on to have a stellar medical career.

As Yogi Berra said:

"That's too coincidental to be a coincidence."

The *Cosmic Coincidence Control Center* is always active in our lives. Think back on your own journey, how many moments, meetings, or narrow misses have quietly steered you toward something greater? Start paying attention. You might be surprised by how often the *Four C's* are already working in your favor. The trick is you have to be wide awake and aware to spot them!

What are the remarkable "coincidences" in your life? I'd love to hear about them. Write to kathleenpasley@hotmail.com to share.

AFFIRMATIONS

How They Work and An Array of Examples

"When we learn to trust the Universe, we shall be happy, prosperous, and well."

- Ernest Holmes

Affirmations are a great reinforcement of the belief that a benign force underlies our world and that this Divine presence wants only the best for each of us. Once we spiritually align ourselves with this Universal force, we can begin to witness our lives unfolding in amazing ways.

Einstein said,

"The only important question is this: Is the

Universe friendly or not?"

A spiritual life and the use of affirmations will help you conclude that it is.

Many of us struggle with a merciless barrage of negative thoughts and self-talk that keeps us stuck listening to old tapes that deliver only negative results. Words are so critical and always help define your life. Many years ago, when I read Louise Hay's book, *You Can Heal Your Life,* for the first time, I started understanding the power of well-chosen words.

In all honesty, I was totally shocked when I first read Louise's words – "You can choose your thoughts." WHAT?! All along, I was assuming that my thoughts picked me, or at best, I had no control over them. In real fact, my ego was in charge. This is not the ego as in "He has an ego as big as the state of Texas" or "I have a healthy ego that helps me keep a positive self-image."

The ego in spiritual terms is a never-ending loop of fear thoughts, jealousy thoughts, discontentment thoughts, me vs. them thoughts and any array of thinking that keeps us in a state of fear, lack, envy, conflict, judgment and disquietude.

In my estimation, the good news is that this ego can be chased away by one simple mind trick – changing your thoughts. Happiness does not depend on what you have or who you are. It solely relies on what you think.

If you truly want to change or improve your life, you must first be willing to change your mind. Louise Hay says:

"Thoughts have no power over us unless we give in to them. Thoughts are only
words strung together...let us choose
to think thoughts that nourish and support us. You are
much more than your mind. You may think your

mind is running the show. But that is only because
you've trained your mind to think in this way. You
can also untrain and train this tool of yours."

I honestly have to say that finally realizing this was the best and most transformative piece of information I ever had the good fortune to stumble across.

Change how you see and see how you change. There isn't anything in this world that can trouble you as much as your own thoughts. A friend of mine used to say that we all have an "itty bitty shitty committee" in our heads that constantly sparks negativity, gloom, criticism and worry. But thoughts can only hold us hostage with our consent. Taking our power back is like no longer giving something or someone rent-free space in our minds.

There's a homeopath in France who is known as Dr. Happiness. He has one simple teaching: At any given moment, he says ask yourself...

"Is the thought that I am currently thinking the happiest thought
I can think? If not, what's the happiest thought
I can think instead?"

One day, as I was walking on the Sanibel beach with my sister, I suggested we engage in an exercise that Louise recommended. Whenever you make a negative statement in a conversation, the other person says "OUT." As we walked along, I couldn't believe how frequently we were saying OUT to each other. It was a real wake-up call as to how often we use negative language without even realizing it!

Affirmations are positive thoughts, ideally expressed in the present tense (such as I am or I have) to deliver positive results. Even if your affirmation seems impossible or silly, you still must state it with conviction. You don't have to believe that affirmations will work; you simply have to practice the discipline on a continuing basis and experience the results.

When you follow your thoughts and the words spoken by you and others throughout the day, you'll find that most of us think in negative affirmations and create more of what we don't want rather than what we do. Saying "I hate my job" will get you nowhere. Declaring, "I now work at the perfect job for me," will open the channels in your consciousness to create just that.

The challenge is to continually make positive statements, in the present tense, about how you want your life to be or what you would like to have happen. If we declare our affirmation in the future tense -- "I want" or "I will have" then that is where that idea will always stay – just out of our reach in the future.

One of the most effective techniques to use when practicing an affirmation is to write it down as well as say it out loud. Each day, take the primary affirmation you are working on and copy it down in long-hand - ten times would be great, but if it's only three times, that would be fine too. Writing in long-hand has a better chance of registering in your subconscious than typing on your computer or simply saying the affirmation out loud. For some reason, the power of writing an affirmation in your journal increases its effectiveness.

In your mind, go over the affirmation whenever you can during the day. For reinforcement, write it down on a notecard and keep it in your pocket or your bag for easy reference. Repetition is the key that allows your unconscious mind, combined with the wisdom of the Universe, to go to work manifesting what you affirm.

Affirmations that you use consistently become beliefs and will produce results, if not immediately, then over time, sometimes in ways you can't even imagine. It makes no difference how negative your life has been or how many mistakes you have made; the Universe wants you to rise triumphantly.

The negativity of all your yesterdays can vanish into nothingness when you consciously guard your thoughts and speech and keep your mind focused on the positive... There is a spiritual power that wants to work with you, and affirmations are one of the keys to opening this channel of Divine goodness and happiness.

The following simple affirmation is the one I use daily whenever I think of it (usually silently). It always makes me feel peaceful and under God's protection.

"I am being divinely guided and protected,

and my life is made smooth and easy."

Here are some ideas for an array of affirmations. You can adapt any of these to your own individual voice, style, and needs. Speak them out loud. Write them down. Reflect on them throughout your day. Let them become a loving part of your inner dialogue.

For General Well-Being

I treat myself with great respect, I treat others with great respect, and I am treated by others with great respect.

Today I feel enriched, empowered, and emboldened.

I am competent, confident, and committed.

I am vibrant, radiant, and joyful.

In the midst of turmoil, I feel calm.

Peace is the order of my day.

I welcome into my life: health, harmony, happiness, and success.

Today, I consciously let go of any discord.

Freedom and joy are mine today.

I am fully alive, filled with love, joy, and gratitude.

Today, I trust in Divine timing. I accept that everything in my life is unfolding for my greatest good. All is well.

I always float downstream rather than fighting to swim upstream.

Everything in my life is unfolding for my greatest good.

To Welcome Good into Your Life

I remember only the good. I accept only the good. I expect only the good. This is all I experience.

Everything always turns out well in my life.

There is good enough to go around.

I am an outlet of immeasurable good.

I am in complete unity with my good.

I know that good is the basic principle of my existence.

For Manifesting Your Dreams

Today, I align myself with the best ways and means of accomplishing my dreams.

Today, I know that all things are possible with God. I move easily and effortlessly from success to success.

I keep on "keeping on" in the direction of my dreams.

I expect the best for myself and the guidance to achieve it

For Finding New and Satisfying Work

I am being divinely guided to the perfect opportunity for using my unique skills for my highest good and that of the Universe.

I am attracting the perfect job that I can feel passionate about, making (Fill in Dollar Amount) or more.

I am of maximum service in my work, making a good living.

My work (my project, my creative endeavor, my report, etc.) is unfolding in ways I couldn't even imagine.

For Finding New Relationships or Improving Current Ones

I am now attracting the perfect relationship into my life.

I live in harmony and balance with (insert name) and everyone I know.

I love myself and treat myself the way I treat others.

I have peaceful relationships in my life.

Friendship, peace, joy, and goodness are mine now and forever.

I surround myself with loving people who see only the good in me.

For Prosperity

I am a magnet for abundance in my life.

I attract money and prosperity easily and effortlessly.

What is needed is on its way.

I identify myself with abundance and success.

For Vibrant Health

I am radiantly healthy and take care of my body with love and respect.

Each cell in my body has Divine Intelligence.

I choose to be healthy and free.

I now claim health instead of sickness.

I sleep in peace, wake in joy, and live in the consciousness of the good.

A Powerful Affirmation for Finding the Right Job

I was visiting friends in Nova Scotia and had recently begun thinking that I wanted to change my job. I decided to dedicate some of my vacation time to contemplating and imagining what that new job might look like. I was struggling with constructing a picture in my mind about how this change would take place and what I had to do to make it happen.

Finally, I landed on the idea of using an affirmation to attract the right work to me. Rather than racking my brain to come up with the penultimate idea, it suddenly made sense to leave it to God, my Higher Self, the Divine Energy, and to be led to the best job possible for me at this point in my career.

The affirmation I wrote out in a spiral-bound notebook was:

"I am being divinely guided to the perfect opportunity for using my unique skills for my highest good and that of the Universe."

To this day, I believe I was guided to scribble down that sentence – it came out so quickly and clearly for me. I'm convinced that including the phrase "for the highest good of myself and that of the Universe" is what made it so powerful. While in Canada, I wrote this affirmation down faithfully ten times a day. I continued this when I returned home and put it in the hands of God.

Crazy as it may sound, the best project I ever worked on dropped into my lap within a month. It had to do with raising money to educate people about AIDS. I had no clue this opportunity would come out of nowhere, with no advance planning on my part. The project used all my marketing, communications, writing, public relations, and selling abilities, plus I felt that it was the opportunity of a lifetime to do something meaningful that meant the world to me.

A Powerful Affirmation for Finding Your Perfect Home

I was looking for a home to purchase in the Georgetown section of Washington, D.C. Georgetown is a beautiful and charming place to live, but many of the homes have quirky or undesirable aspects to them, not to mention they can be extraordinarily expensive! I was searching for about a week when I went to an open house for a historic townhouse.

Perfect location… check!

Charming interior… check!

Recently renovated… check!

Great kitchen… check!

The right number of bedrooms… check!

And a beautiful garden… double check!!

I danced home that afternoon, congratulating myself on finding my perfect "dream house." I was a bit nervous about making this large a purchase, so I didn't get back to the realtor until the next day. Lo and behold, I had dragged my feet too long, and it had already sold. Drat!

For the next two months, I trudged around all of Georgetown to look at any houses that were for sale. The whole time, I was beating up on myself, saying: "I lost my dream house; I lost my dream house!"

Suddenly, I stopped dead in my tracks, realizing that I considered myself to be the Affirmation Queen of D.C. and an avid proponent of positive thinking.

So, I started affirming:

"My perfect house is coming to me. My perfect house is coming to me!"

Guess what? The very next day, I attended yet one more open house and met a realtor I had never seen before. When I told her what I was looking for, she told me that another home was coming on the market the very next day, and would I like to take an advance peek?

Fast forward, this was indeed the PERFECT home for me: 125 years old, newly renovated, two living rooms, two fireplaces, a huge picture window looking out on a walled-in brick garden, complete with a huge and gorgeous cherry blossom tree rounding out the appeal. I was ecstatic, purchased it that day, and loved living there for a full 23 years!

There is absolutely no doubt in my mind that I was divinely guided in both these examples. I simply had to get out of my own way, affirm what I wanted, and let the Universe do the rest.

AN ATTITUDE OF GRATITUDE

Brings More to Be Grateful For

"If you look to others for fulfillment,

You will never truly be fulfilled.

If your happiness depends on money,

You will never be happy` with yourself.

Be content with what you have.

Rejoice in the way things are.

When you realize nothing is lacking,

The whole world belongs to you."

- Lao Tzu

All spiritual paths emphasize the importance of gratitude, especially for the simple things in life. Gratitude is a spiritual discipline, a stunningly simple practice, but one that is not always easy.

It's all well and good to give a big and enthusiastic THANK YOU to the Universe when you're on top of the world, but what about those days when your life seems like one big mess, things aren't going well, and you wake up with that dreaded feeling: Oh NO… another day!? These are the times, in fact, when we need a particularly large dose of gratitude.

When we focus on all we have to be thankful for, our lives feel abundant; when we focus on resentments and what's missing, our lives feel lacking and empty. What we choose to focus on is what we usually get.

M.J. Ryan, in her book *Attitudes of Gratitude*, says:

"As we get older, we get schooled in our mistakes, and learn to focus on what's not right, what is lacking, missing, inadequate, and painful. That's why gratitude is so powerful. It helps us to return to our natural state of joyfulness, where we notice what's right instead of what's wrong. Gratitude reminds us to be like plants, which turn toward, not away from, the light."

The wonderful thing about gratitude is that it is impossible to feel the positive emotion of thankfulness at the same time you are feeling a negative emotion, such as anger. Just the mere act of shifting your mind to feeling thankful for something or someone dissolves fear, anger, jealousy, resentment, and bitterness, seemingly without effort.

Gratitude works like a magnet and attracts more things to be grateful for. It does this by transforming your energy frequency to a higher level and then attracting other people and situations that resonate at that higher frequency.

The Dalai Lama says:

"One positive thought in the morning can change your whole day."

In my experience, you don't have to wake up thankful for the whole kit and caboodle. But the biggest favor you can do for yourself each morning is to think about something you can see as a blessing.

Recognizing all you have to be thankful for, even during the worst times of your life, sets the vibration for better things to come. It is not the ups and downs that happen to us that make or break us; it is the way we think about them. As the expression goes, it is not happy people who are thankful. It is thankful people who are happy.

I'm a huge fan of writing out a gratitude list every morning. You can start with three items and then extend the practice to fill a page of a small journal every day. My journals are inexpensive and are purchased on Amazon. You can go high-end, spending $50.00 or more, or purchase one for around $7.00. The most economical way to buy journals is in a three-pack.

I've been writing out a gratitude list in the morning for years and find, on most days, it keeps me "on the sunny side of the street." This is a practice that helps on ordinary days as well as in our darkest hours.

Some prefer to round out their evening with a deliberate pause before going to bed, reflecting on the positive aspects of their day. Best of all is to do both morning and night, but for me, committing to a morning ritual has worked best.

Here are a few tips:

Don't overthink it. Using a flow of consciousness makes for a sincere and authentic gratitude list.

Write down your list, starting each item with "Thank you, God," "the Divine Presence," or "the Universal Force." In other words, replace the word God with whatever moniker is most comfortable for you.

Another way to frame your gratitude list is the way I choose to do it - to write your list as a letter, starting with "Dear God," and then list each item as a phrase, such as things and people in everyday life:

Thank you for my sleep. Thank you for my girlfriends, Sue, Carol, Anne, Phylis, Herta, Colleen, Andrea, Robin and Rose. Thank you for my job. Thank you for my family. Thank you for my book group. Thank you for pizza. Thank you for yesterday's game of golf.

Here are some other examples to give you the gist of it:

Acknowledge things that you appreciate about your world: Thank you for my house. Thank you for my job. Thank you for my car, etc.

Mention your talents and gifts: Thank you for my creativity. Thank you for my ability to love deeply. Thank you for my sense of humor, etc.

Think of all the help God gives you so graciously every day: Thank you for your guidance. Thank you for watching over me. Thank you for your acceptance of me. Thank you for ALL. Thank you for YOU in my life, etc.

Think of the small and big things in life: Thank you for my health. Thank you for music. Thank you for my love of reading. Thank you for my trip to France. Thank you for my gratitude list. Thank you for all the adventures I've had in my life, etc.

General: Thank you for Nature. Thank you for my garden. Thank you for keeping my family safe. The possibilities are endless.

As you continue in your gratitude practice, you will naturally come up with unique parts of life and events to be grateful for, which is why I never get tired of writing them.

You will also start finding yourself noticing, throughout your day, all the little events, small pleasures, and simple wonders around you that make you stop and be grateful in the moment. Your gratitude muscles just naturally strengthen with use.

Don't forget to take a few seconds before you go to sleep at night to thank God for the day. I just do this verbally (that is, if I remember!)

Here's an additional time to express gratitude. Karen Casey, in her daily reading book, *Each Day a New Beginning,* suggests that when we're feeling self-pity, anger, or overwhelming fear, making a gratitude list can quickly change how we experience our lives in that moment. If we want a new experience, we must do our part to cultivate a different attitude.

Thaddeus Golas said:

"Inside yourself or outside, you never have to change

what you see, only the way you see it."

Another important technique, but a more difficult one, when using gratitude as a spiritual practice, is to contemplate those situations in your life that are most difficult as well as those difficult people in your life who you have the most problems with, and express gratitude to them.

They are your teachers, and as you stretch yourself to feel appreciation for them, hard as it may seem, you will find your heavy feelings lifting. As with forgiveness, you can pretend you are grateful, even if you can't feel sincerely grateful at the time. It will eventually come.

Gratitude can be combined with affirmations in order to manifest what you want. Here's how this method works: identify two things that you are already thankful for and describe how these gifts in your life make you feel. The more specific and visual you can be about those things you are grateful for now, the better. Then identify two things you want that you don't yet have.

Here's an example:

Already Have:

1. I am so thankful to the Universe for my beautiful garden that blooms every spring and makes me feel so peaceful.

2. I am so thankful to the Universe for my two wonderful children, who make me feel so joyful and fulfilled.

Hope to Have:

3. I am so thankful to the Universe for my healthy, fun, supportive, and humor-filled relationship that brings me so much pleasure and opportunities to express love.

4. I am so thankful to the Universe for my wonderful job that endlessly utilizes my creativity and skills among colleagues I like, in a supportive environment, at a generous salary.

Gratitude is a habit that helps us cultivate positive emotions. The more grateful we are, the more love we feel, the more joy we experience, and the more compassion we express.

It helps us to notice what is right instead of what is wrong. It makes us feel whole—at least for the moment—and confident that we have everything we need as we go through the day.

As Brian Tracy says:

"Develop an attitude of gratitude, and give thanks for everything that happens to you, knowing that every step forward is a step toward achieving something bigger and better than your current situation."

When It's Difficult to Think of Anything to be Thankful For

My uber-spiritual friend, Julie, told a friend of hers, who at the time was always in turmoil and seemed to move from one disaster to another, that she should get out of bed in the morning and immediately think: "I'm thankful for my legs."

That really stuck with me as brilliant because there is always something to be grateful for. On some days, I have to start with the simplest of things: a cup of coffee, a bird chirping, a tree outside the window, a soft bed, running water, a good night's sleep, and on and on. I learned a new one during the pandemic: elastic waistbands!

Gratitude for A Person You Resent

A few years back, I had an experience around feeling resentful toward a man I had been involved with in my late twenties and early thirties. It was a very co-dependent relationship and really stymied my growth for a number of years. I swear, I hadn't thought about him in years when I started telling a friend about this ill-fated romance.

Suddenly, I experienced complete rage toward Russell and would have strangled him with my bare hands if he had appeared in my living room. My resentments loomed large, and I recognized that I still had work to do to let go of my negative feelings around this relationship—feelings that were so buried, I didn't even know I had them!

That night, I experienced a great deal of turmoil and anger, tossing from side to side all through my sleep. When I woke up, I had the flash of a thought: "Take the best and leave the rest."

How to transform lingering anger and resentment about a past relationship? Hold on to your appreciation and leave the regrets behind. Bless the other person, yourself, and the relationship for the gifts you received and the experience through which you grew. By the end of that day of giving thanks for Russell, all I could think of was the fun we had, all the things I learned from him, and the love we had shared. It was VERY freeing.

In the land of Divine order, all experiences are blessings. Just for today, choose acceptance and gratitude in all situations. The secret to having it all is knowing that you already do.

I am a big fan of the Irish singer Enya. In one of her songs, she repeats in the refrain:

"On my way home, I'll remember only good things."

These days, that's my mantra. It can be yours too!

FORGIVENESS

The Key to Happiness

"Whenever you feel that someone has injured you, or sullied your reputation, or caused you physical harm, the spiritual solution, as difficult as it may appear, is to extend forgiveness. To hold onto the pain and seek to exact revenge will simply keep you stuck in pain, and the problem will be exacerbated."

- Wayne Dyer

When we are judgmental or unbending in holding onto offenses, we are the ones who suffer. As the expression goes, holding onto a resentment is like pouring the other person a cup of poison and drinking it yourself.

Why do we need to forgive? Because it is the way we experience the compassion that we want God to show to us; it is the way advocated by all spiritual traditions and religions; and it is the spiritual way in which we discover unconditional love. Who do you need to forgive? The pathway to love is always through forgiveness.

There are certainly times when you hope someone will forgive you. "I'm sorry. Please forgive me." are the five most powerful words you have in your apology arsenal! And, of course, these are often the toughest words in the English language to say (and mean!) when you've had an argument, experienced a misunderstanding, or hurt someone.

Back to when you need to forgive someone else. The mantra many of us use when we feel particularly aggrieved? "I'll forgive, but I'll never forget." Sorry, that does not constitute real forgiveness!

My focus here is not on those minor league spats that can be resolved within a few hours or days. The true challenge is to deal with those unforgiving thoughts that we've told ourselves are totally justifiable, or resentments that we've held onto, sometimes for years. This can be with someone who is alive or someone who has passed away—a family member, a lover, a friend, a co-worker, or even yourself. The list is endless.

Be that as it may, no matter what your spiritual inclination...the central tenet of any religion or spiritual practice is always love, compassion, and of course: FORGIVENESS.

In our spiritual work (and it IS work), forgiveness is the toughest task. Yet it is the most important thing we can do for ourselves, never mind the other person!

Byron Katie says:

"Forgiveness is just another word for freedom."

YOUR freedom is what she means here. No, it's not about doing the other person a big favor—it's shedding the burden for YOU and letting go of thoughts that might have eaten away at you for years. The accompaniment to being unforgiving is always resentment.

If you're honest with yourself, there's probably more than one person you need to forgive. Forgiveness can sometimes feel more painful than the original wound suffered. And yet, there is no peace of mind without forgiveness. *A Course in Miracles* (ACIM) helps us to ask the question: "Would I rather be right or would I rather be happy?"

ACIM goes so far as to say:

"Forgiveness is the key to happiness."

In my personal experience, I have found that forgiveness is a process, not a single event, one that can take time, and that you can't push your way through. It doesn't work to say: "Abracadabra… Now I forgive you, and all is well." And it doesn't help to say a hollow "You're forgiven," when that is clearly not the truth.

To forgive is to set a prisoner free—and discover that the prisoner is you.

The strange thing about letting go of a grievance is that once you have really forgiven a person, the heavily charged feelings of anger, resentment, hurt, betrayal, blame, and self-righteousness often lift completely, and it becomes almost impossible to remember what it was to experience such venomous feelings.

But until we reach that critical point of fully forgiving, it is virtually impossible to imagine letting the pain go and extending an olive branch.

Forgiveness is a process, not a one-time event. Over time, forgiveness results in powerful personal and planetary healing. When we forgive, we don't change the past, but we change our futures. What changes is your future and the person you forgive, whether you witness this change or not. When we are forgiving, we are most like God, who continually pours out mercy on each of us.

As you work with forgiveness, don't forget to forgive yourself. Allow yourself the gifts of freedom, strength, and peace of mind: FORGIVE.

Here are a couple of techniques that might work for you. In extending forgiveness to those whom we think have hurt us, we open ourselves to a new kind of connection with them, as well as with others.

Forgiveness Exercise #1

Put pen to paper and write a letter (that you never plan to send), laying out all your grievances and why you were so deeply hurt by this person. A particularly powerful way to do this, especially with a parent, is to write the letter using your non-dominant hand. The result will be that your handwriting looks like the work of a first grader. It will also slow down your writing to a snail's pace, allowing a flood of memories to come back to you.

Before you sign your letter, simply write at least three times in your normal handwriting:

I forgive you; I release you; I release myself.

I forgive you; I release you; I release myself.

I forgive you; I release you; I release myself.

Do this even if it doesn't feel sincere. Repeat as often as it takes to feel your spirit lifting and the resentment dissolving.

Forgiveness Exercise #2

You can say the following out loud, or, if you want to make it even more powerful, say it to another person who is standing in for the person you are working to forgive. Fill in the blank in vivid detail:

I can't forgive you because you did the following to me:

_____

Visualize the person and say at least five times:

I ask for the same happiness for you that I want for myself.

Easy Forgiveness: Exercise #3

Sit quietly with your eyes closed and say:

The person I need to forgive is _____, and I forgive you for _____.

Imagine the person you are forgiving saying to you: "Thank you, I set you free now."

The most powerful way to do this is to spend five minutes repeating it over and over. Try it, you're worth the time it takes.

Easiest of All Exercise #4

PRAY, PRAY, PRAY for the person you need to forgive, releasing him or her to God. Knowing that wishing someone the best, if you can possibly do it, is the most healing thing you can do for yourself.

These exercises can be so difficult to do because you may feel like a fake, an impostor... that nothing is going to change your negative feelings about this person.

Remember the slogan:

"I am only as big as the smallest thing that

I hold in unforgiveness."

The pathway to love is forgiveness. Forgiveness is the way that we experience the compassion and mercy that we want God to show us.

Mahatma Gandhi said:

"The weak can never forgive. Forgiveness

is an attribute of the strong."

When we are resentful and harbor hatred, we are stuck at a very low vibrational level. To free ourselves and move past our unforgiving thoughts, we often must go through a process over time. While you can't pretend to forgive before you are ready, you can exercise your forgiveness muscles even while you still harbor resentments that don't seem possible to lessen.

Nothing necessarily needs to be done with the other person directly. In fact, even though you may never see or talk to that person again, both of you will still gain the benefits of spiritual healing.

In extending forgiveness to those whom we think have hurt us, we open ourselves to a new kind of connection with them, as well as with others. The strange thing about letting go of a grievance is that once you have really forgiven a person, the heavily charged feelings of anger, resentment, hurt, betrayal, blame, and self-righteousness often lift completely, and it becomes almost impossible to remember what it was like to experience such venomous feelings.

My best definition of God Himself is mercy, unconditional love, grace, and the Divine Presence who "cuts us some slack." So why is it so hard for us to have this same kind of tolerance?

Until we reach that critical point of being able to fully forgive, it is virtually impossible to imagine letting the pain go and extending an olive branch.

Let's use the example of Jesus. His greatest achievement, in my mind, was to show us that despite being reviled, tortured, beaten, brutalized, and humiliated by his tormentors (after doing nothing but good deeds!), he still had forgiveness in his heart.

When we are forgiving, we are most like God, who continually pours out mercy on each of us. As you work with forgiveness, don't forget to forgive yourself. Allow yourself the gifts of freedom, strength, and peace of mind: FORGIVE.

Forgiving a Parent Who Has Passed Away

One of the most powerful forgiveness processes I have ever experienced took place in a single day at a workshop in Boston. It was called "Healing Your Father Wounds" and was led by John Bradshaw, a well-known author and speaker on family systems and their impact on individuals. He appeared often on PBS in the 1980s and 1990s to support their fundraising efforts but has since passed away.

The program took place in a large center that fit about 150 people, and the place was packed. I realized then that holding onto a father wound was not as rare as I thought.

In my case, my wound wasn't due to any behavior by my father. I was extremely close to him—he was an exceptional man. Not only brilliant (a Princeton man), a successful businessman (the treasurer of a major Fortune 500 company), but also very handsome and kind.

He tragically died at the age of 47 from brain cancer...I was just 14 years old, the day before his death. He had struggled with his illness for about two years. The real kicker was that I had a sister who was 18 at the time, a brother who was four, and another brother who was one. No matter which ages we fell into, it was hard on us all, both short and long term.

My mother was agoraphobic—an anxiety disorder characterized by an intense and persistent fear of being in situations where escape might be difficult or help might not be available. She also had panic disorder, with a fear of enclosed spaces (such as stores), crowds, and was vulnerable to having a panic attack at any time. Each of her children, as soon as they could see over a shopping cart, would do the grocery shopping for the family!

Believe it or not, my mother was a delightful person and a good parent in many ways, with a terrific sense of humor. Unfortunately, her mental handicaps made it difficult for her to function well as a single parent. Consequently, my sister and I were very involved with bringing up my younger brothers.

To give you a sense of the age difference: the youngest of my two brothers was in kindergarten when I was a freshman in college! When my sister married when I was sixteen, my responsibilities became even more intense.

So, back to the workshop on healing your father wounds. The most powerful exercise we did occurred when we divided into circles of about seven people. Each of us wrote a letter to our father using the non-dominant hand, which required a slow pace and resulted in childlike handwriting plus a surprisingly real feeling of being a kid again. We were asked to write a letter (not to be sent) that told our father the things we needed from him and never received. Then we read them aloud to the group.

As expected, there was a tremendous amount of crying and sobbing in the room as we carried out this exercise. One of my friends was so upset, he left the event. The rest of the program is a blur to me but writing that letter is indelibly cemented in my mind.

I was shocked at how angry I was at my father for leaving us, especially given my mother's limitations. I was also shocked by how much forgiveness work I still had to do around my father and his death. Even though he obviously didn't have any control over his fatal illness, my feelings weren't based on logic, but on wounded emotions.

After that letter-writing experience, I felt a great weight lifted from my shoulders. Do I still miss my father after all these years? Yes, of course. Do I still have issues over his dying at such a young age, with a lingering illness? You bet. But I learned how to forgive him on that special day with John Bradshaw, and it felt WONDERFUL.

An Unforgiven Person Can Turn Into a Friend

In my late 30s, when I still lived in Boston, I had a business partner who was brilliant and a marketing genius. Ellen and I made a great team, and with the two of us, our business was thriving. But she suddenly decided that she wanted to go off and start her own company. I felt completely deserted, not to mention mad as a hornet, that she gave me no notice. It felt like she completely left me and the company in the lurch. Then she tried to steal away my best employee, which enraged me even further!

By that time, I was a few years into my spiritual studies and knew that forgiveness was a key to happiness. I didn't want to feel such resentment and murderous thoughts, but I couldn't talk myself down from them. One day, I was walking through the Boston Commons (a large Boston park) on my way to work. I kept ruminating about how I was ever going to forgive this woman.

Suddenly, a little voice in my head said that I could forgive Ellen, but I NEVER had to see or talk to her again. That completely took the edge off my emotional turmoil, and with the passage of time, I realized I had naturally forgiven her and felt no grudge.

Fast forward ten years. I was now living in Washington, DC, working as a marketing consultant. One day, the phone rang, and it was

Ellen. She called to ask if I could commute to Boston to help her with her business four days a week.

I almost fainted, but I needed the work and said yes. I stayed at her house every time I went to Boston, and she went all out to create a wonderful space for me. My bedroom looked like a princess's room, and she treated me like a queen.

What I had read about in all my spiritual studies had manifested: when you forgive someone, even if it takes ten years to do so—there is a healing that takes place for both parties.

Ellen and I have remained friends, with no animosity or residual anger. In fact, I consider her to be a very close friend. Wow! These spiritual practices really DO work.

AHA! MOMENTS

When That Lightbulb Goes On

Merriam-Webster defines an Aha! Moment as: "A moment of sudden realization, inspiration, insight, recognition, or comprehension."

I've had a number of these over the years, as most of us have, but a few stand out more than others. Interestingly, many of my powerful Aha! Experiences came during therapy. Actually, they often hit me after the session, when I was walking home or reflecting quietly, suddenly thinking, "Wow. Now there was a real insight into such-and-such." And from that point forward, the realization stayed with me, becoming part of how I lived and understood the world.

Michael Neill, in his book *The Inside-Out Revolution*, puts it beautifully:

"Insights are those wonderful 'Aha!' moments when we can see something about ourselves, our life, or life itself in a brand-new way. People often call them 'light-bulb moments' because we see things in a new light that makes them look less fixed and less scary than before. In these wonderful, transformational moments,

we discover a fresh way of seeing something. We suddenly get it, not

intellectually, but at an almost cellular level. Quite simply,

A Revelation in India

The biggest Aha! Moment of my life happened over a decade ago in India. It was a serious "light-bulb moment", an eye-popping, mind-bending experience that certainly changed how I see the world.

I was on a two-week journey led by our retreat leader, Edemir, to northern India with a group of fellow seekers. Our first destination was Rishikesh, a small spiritual city nestled in the Himalayan foothills. Known as the birthplace of yoga, Rishikesh is also famous for hosting the Beatles more than 50 years ago, when they studied Transcendental Meditation with Maharishi Mahesh Yogi.

Temples and ashrams line the banks of the Ganges River in Rishikesh. Every morning at 4:30 a.m. (definitely not my favorite time of day!), we visited a particular temple to meditate and soak in the sacred energy so integral to the Hindu tradition.

Rishikesh is completely vegetarian and alcohol-free. There are no cars, just tuk-tuks, which sit two people and a driver in something like a small electric rickshaw. So, it is primarily a walking city where most travel happens on foot. The two sides of the city are linked by a rather shaky walking bridge over the Ganges that had me terrorized every time I had to walk over it!

The only real downside to this leg of our journey was the roughness of the accommodations. The rooms were less than basic. The beds were wooden with straw mattresses, nearly impossible to sleep on. The "shower" consisted of a bucket and a spigot in the corner of the room.

Of course, I promptly booked an appointment at a hairdresser's so I could at least have my hair washed. (Always one for modern comforts!) And guess what they used in this so-called salon? A bucket and a spigot, of course.

One day, while walking alone, I wandered into a lovely but modest home that was open to the public. To Western eyes, much of India appears chaotic and unkempt, but this place was spotless and serene. It had belonged to Swami Chidananda, a guru who had passed away in 2008. His home was peaceful, adorned with fresh flowers and infused with quiet, sacred energy.

As I explored room to room, I entered his bedroom. The bed was neatly made, a well-worn wheelchair sat nearby, and his slippers were carefully placed next to it. While Chidananda had been dead for years, the space felt as if he had just stepped out.

In another room, I came upon a huge, framed photograph of the guru hung on the far wall. His face radiated peace, serenity, and warmth. I stood there gazing at him...and then something remarkable happened. His face began to shift.

One after another, new faces appeared in rapid succession, each one unique, unfamiliar, constantly transforming. It felt as if Swami Chidananda was revealing the essence of humanity itself, that all of us are one. His face became a tapestry of countless others, flowing from one to the next. I kept blinking, shaking my head, trying to refocus. But the shifting faces continued. It was as though all of humanity was reflected in this single, holy image.

I wasn't sure whether to feel awed or alarmed. On one level, it felt like a spiritual funhouse; on another, a sacred glimpse into the mystical. I wondered if I was hallucinating, but I promise, there were no drugs involved!

I ran back to our lodging and practically dragged Edemir, back to the house. When we arrived and stepped into the room with the portrait…nothing happened. Just a photo of a kind-looking man in a simple orange robe. No visions, no shifting faces. And yet, I've never for a minute doubted what I saw.

So, what was my Aha! Takeaway from that experience? I had three:

1. There are dimensions beyond this material world that I know absolutely nothing about.

2. Though our identities may appear different, we are all the same. We are truly and profoundly ALL ONE.

3. Mysteries abound, and I may never understand them while walking this earth in human skin. But I am deeply grateful for the moments when I do catch a glimpse of the mysterious and unknown, reminding me of what Shakespeare wrote in one of Hamlet's speeches: "There are more things in Heaven and Earth, Horatio, than are dreamt of in your philosophy."

An Experience with an Earthly Angel

I was looking forward to a trip to Brazil for the wedding of Edemir's son. I was traveling with two friends, gathering my things and getting ready to head to the airport, when, about an hour before we were due to leave, I opened my passport and to my horror...it had been expired! I have no idea how I missed it, since I was traveling frequently in those days. I did have an up-to-date Brazilian visa, so I may have just looked at that. Regardless, what a dilemma!

My girlfriends and I decided that I'd still go to Dulles Airport with them, just to see if, by some miracle, I might be able to get on the plane. Lo and behold, the check-in agent at United missed the expiration date, and I happily boarded the flight. Whew!

But as soon as we were airborne, the reality hit: I was about to have a big problem getting through customs in São Paulo. Being a firm believer in prayer, I started sending up urgent pleas to God. Then I switched my tactic to pray to Archangel Gabriel. A few weeks earlier, Edemir had taught a class on the Archangels, and since Gabriel was the messenger angel—famous for telling Mary she would give birth to Jesus—he's always depicted with a trumpet and is considered the angel of communications. I prayed he'd help me find the right words to talk my way through customs!

Moving up in the line, I kept praying to Gabriel for help with the customs official. Well, that didn't work, and I was told I'd have to return to the States on the next flight! My friends, Julie, Lisa, and I huddled together to figure out what to do next. A very kind and calm United

Airlines employee approached us to see if he could help with my obvious predicament and the commotion I was causing.

I explained that if I missed this wedding, my friend would never forgive me. He told us there was only one possible solution: my friends would need to drive across the city on a one-and-a-half-hour ride to the U.S. Consulate and try to get me a temporary passport. They had to do this without me since I wasn't allowed to leave the customs area without a passport. Shooting me some dirty looks (who could blame them?), off went Julie and Lisa to hail a taxi and brave the city traffic for three hours for the round trip to the Consulate.

Meanwhile, my new friend from United Airlines offered to take me to the United Polaris Lounge for V.I.P. travelers. I drank some champagne, a little lunch, and sampled the wonderful chocolates being offered. I read my book, took a nap, and tried not to feel *too* guilty about my friends schlepping across São Paulo because of my oversight.

Eventually, they returned with my one-year temporary passport in hand. Eureka! Victory! As my United Airlines friend and I walked down the hallway to meet Julie and Lisa, it suddenly occurred to me that I didn't even know his name. I asked.

He smiled and said, "Gabriel."

I almost fainted.

A Heavenly Visit

This story is one of the most memorable of my life and the one that gives me goosebumps even thinking about it today. In fact, I hesitated to include this particular memory in this book because it sounds so outlandish and hard to believe. But I know it happened...I had a celestial visit to assuage my misery when suffering from a major depression.

Because I only expected to be there for six months, the first house in Washington, DC that I lived in was incredibly small. Fitting one extra person in my living room was a real challenge! It was so small, I had to hang my coat on the back of the front door! Since I'm a very social person, this would normally be a problem. However, I didn't care that I was living in such a small place because I was deeply depressed and didn't want to see people anyway. Whenever I experience depression, I prefer to be alone.

I was crying, more like sobbing, in my bedroom, tossing and turning in misery on my bed. Suddenly, I felt a presence pinning my shoulders to the bed. I know it sounds kind of crazy, but I believe it was an angel. I never saw him, but I will never forget what he had to say.

It was a male voice that talked to me out loud with one very brief, sentence-long message. I never heard a voice before or since, but his talking to me was as real as someone standing next to me, giving me some valuable advice. I never saw anything, but he said with a gentle but firm voice:

"YOU HAVE TO QUIET YOUR MIND
IN ORDER TO HEAR."

Then the presence left as quickly as it had made itself known. My first thought was that the voice was advising me to start to seriously meditate. But as time has gone by and I have become more knowledgeable about spirituality, my opinion has changed.

I believe that the angel was advising me that Divine guidance comes to a quiet mind, not an unquiet one. I believe that the "small voice" within requires devoting some silent time to hearing its gentle messages and intuitions. I believe that the voice is always coming from a loving place, and you can't lose if you quiet your mind long enough to hear it!

When I was depressed, my mind was anything but quiet. I constantly ruminated about the horrible mistakes I made in the past and then projected misery and fear into the future. Those of you who have experienced a serious depression will know what I'm talking about. When you go deeply into a depression, it's almost impossible to shake feelings of hopelessness about the future and regrets about the past. Winston Churchill suffered from episodic dark moods, and he called the experience the "black dog." I call it the 'black lagoon." Both are very fitting descriptions!

I quickly overcame my depression after that celestial visit. How can one be depressed when you've been blessed to receive a direct message from the Heavens? And I have tried to remember that simple message ever since.

INTUITION

You Need Frequent Check-Ins

"I think we all have a little voice inside us that will guide us... If we shut out all the noise and clutter from our lives and listen to that voice, it will tell us the right thing to do."

- Christopher Reeve

Intuition is simply listening to what your spirit has to say—or, as H.P. Blavatsky put it, "following the instinct of the soul." It's knowing something without knowing how you know it. Intuitive knowledge comes to us spontaneously and directly, bypassing logic and reason. When we tap into our spiritual senses, we access emotional awareness and inner knowing, rather than just intellectual analysis.

Author Shakti Gawain once wrote:

"For most of us, the practice of allowing our intuition to guide us is really a new way of life, very different from what we have been taught in the past. If we have been conditioned to approach life entirely rationally—to follow rules or to do what we think others want—then beginning to follow our own inner truth is a major shift."

Louise Hay called her intuition an "inner ding." I call it the small voice within. You might know it as a hunch, a gut feeling, or an inner knowing. Regardless of what you call it, that unexpected nudge in your belly—the one you can't explain—in my view, means that you are being tapped on the shoulder by the Universal Force, God, your Guardian Angel, or whatever you care to call it. You don't need to label it. You just need to listen.

When our habit is to think about every little thing in our lives through the lens of the rational mind, we usually go through life trying to control the outcome of every detail. As we start listening more to our intuition, we stop trying to always figure things out in our heads. We can even wait for things to unfold naturally, trusting that the outcome might not be known by us, but feeling confident that it will be for our best if directed by the Universe. Because intuition is connected to both our soul and Universal Intelligence, it is always guiding us towards the highest good for ourselves and for others.

As I've gotten older, I've learned to trust that "inner ding" more than ever. It never lies. But I'll admit—I've often ignored it, questioned it, dismissed it, or overridden it... usually at my own peril!

Bottom line? Always listen to that little voice in the back of your head. If necessary, put that reliable little guy on speakerphone! Intuition is more than just a feeling; it's one of the clearest, most trustworthy guides we have and will never lead you astray.

NOTE TO SELF

I told you so.

Sincerely,

Your Intuition

When it comes to faith in our intuition, we're in good company. Many of the most admired and brilliant minds in history have said the same.

Steve Jobs once said:

"Intuition is a powerful thing, more powerful than the intellect."

Albert Einstein echoed this sentiment with his own remarkable insight:

"The intellect has little to do on the road to discovery. There comes a leap in consciousness. Call it Intuition or what you will, the solution comes

to you, and you don't know how or why."

And perhaps most famously from Einstein:

"The intuitive mind is a sacred gift, and the rational mind

is a faithful servant. We have created a society that

honors the servant and has forgotten the gift."

Jonas Salk, the medical researcher who developed the polio vaccine, believed:

"Intuition will tell the thinking mind where to look next."

William James, the father of modern psychology, noted:

"Instinct leads. Logic does but follow."

All intuition comes from a Divine Energy that each and every one of us has within us. It is a sacred gift and the best path for figuring out anything that is a challenge in our lives. Train yourself to always listen to it!

Krishnamurti described it beautifully:

"Intuition is the whisper of the soul."

Wayne Dyer wrote:

"If prayer is you talking to God, then intuition is

God talking to you."

Gary Zukav put it in practical terms:

"Intuition is a walkie-talkie between the personality and the soul."

Each of these quotes is a reminder that intuition is not something we develop from the outside, it's something we remember from within. It's always been there. And when we begin to trust it, we begin to walk hand-in-hand with the Divine.

Longing to be your most intuitive self? Here's what Travis Bradberry wrote about learning from highly intuitive people:

Six Things the Most Intuitive People Do

Differently Than the Rest of Us

1. They slow down enough to hear their inner voice.

2. They always listen to their gut feeling instead of dismissing or doubting it.

3. They practice empathy accuracy, an intuitive awareness of what others are thinking and feeling.

4. They practice mindfulness, being in the moment, and filtering out distractions.

5. They nurture their creativity.

6. They analyze their dreams. Intuitive people don't just think, "Wow, that was a weird dream!" They ask themselves, "Where did that come from, and what can I take away from it?"

Identifying a Charlatan

I never discredit my gut instinct when it comes to human beings. Don't assume you're being paranoid—your body can pick up on bad vibes before your rational mind "gets it." If something inside of you says a person or situation isn't right, trust it.

Years ago, I took a class with a woman who claimed to be a high-level spiritual teacher. I had a very bad vibe from her when I walked into the classroom. When she said she'd been a successful race car driver, a model, a climber of Mount Everest, and an Olympic champion archer, I was getting more and more suspicious. But when she claimed she was the reincarnation of Mary Magdalene, I ran out of the room!

Truth be told, I had a negative feeling about her from the moment I saw her. I should have left the workshop as soon as I arrived. I felt in my bones that she was a charlatan before I even met her. I was oh so right!

A Business Take on Intuition

I worked in the corporate world for many years and witnessed firsthand how intuition is a key ingredient in successful leadership.

Many of the world's most influential businesspeople admit to making major decisions based not on logic or data, but on intuition. One of the best descriptions I've seen comes from William Amelio, former president of Lenovo. He shared the following list of leadership principles, each of which emphasizes the power of trusting your gut:

Strategic:

Focus on a few critical decisions.

A decision is better than no decision, but don't let it run too far if it's not working.

Trust your intuition.

People:

Communicate big decisions regularly and frequently.

Don't tolerate jerks.

Build a team you can trust.

Trust your intuition.

Self:

Get feedback early and often—and act on it.

Earn others' trust and confidence.

Gain credibility by showing your vulnerabilities.

You have strengths; use them.

Trust your intuition.

Never apologize for trusting your "inner ding." Your brain can play tricks, your heart can be blind, but your gut is always right!

PRAYER

Talking to God

"If the only prayer you said in your whole life was 'thank you,' that would suffice."

- Meister Eckhart

Whether you're an atheist, an agnostic, a Jesuit priest, or a spiritually oriented person, we are all praying all day long. The thoughts we think, every word we speak, and everything we do is a prayer. We are at all times connected to the Source (God, the Creator, the Divine, the Universal Energy, etc.). So, whatever is going on, the Universal Force is aware of our deepest needs and wants.

The purpose of deliberate prayer is to align the mind with a higher consciousness and to foster an intimate relationship with God. And that's what I recommend you do every day before you get working on the "to-do" list that is chronically buzzing in your head.

Taking a few minutes each morning to become grounded and connected with the God of your understanding can be a lot more beneficial than another fifteen minutes on the treadmill!

Both prayer and meditation are effective ways to become connected with your Higher Source. The purpose of prayer is to align the mind with the thoughts and the will of God. Meditation is a time of quiet when the mind is freed from its attachment to worldly things. It's been said that prayer is when we talk to God, and meditation is when we listen.

By creating a sacred space for your prayer practice and honoring simple preparation rituals, you will find yourself more committed to the daily work required. The basics you need are very simple: a comfortable private place, a time of silence for yourself, and a determination to make spirituality a central anchoring point of your life.

You can strengthen your morning ritual by lighting a candle. You might also want to designate a specific place to set up an altar for prayer and meditation. The altar could include "power objects"—items that feel special to you, are a source of strength, or provide a sense of peace when you look at them.

An altar helps express your divinity externally and establishes a sacred space. Examples of suitable objects for your altar might be: a picture of Jesus or any avatar, a statue of Buddha, a picture of an angel, a shell from the beach, rocks, crystals, a cross, fresh flowers, Rosary beads, a picture of yourself as a child, a symbol of Nature, a piece of jewelry that has important meaning to you, or an object you brought back from an important trip.

When you settle in for your morning ritual, you might want to put on some soothing, meditative music. There are some good choices under the Spiritual and Soothing Music section at the back of this book. Music serves the purpose of relaxing us and establishing a break from the routine, providing an entryway to a separate, sacred time.

Good advice: pray more and worry less! The two are very often interconnected. When life is rough, pray. When life is great, pray. Do your praying daily, and you might just find your stress and anxiety levels diminishing on their own. You also might realize that, as for most of us, your problems and worries really reside primarily between your ears!

Here are a couple of good examples:

Dear God,

"My prayer in this coming year

is a fat bank account and a thin body.

But please don't mix them up

like you did last year.

and

God finally answered my prayers for

winning the lottery.

The answer is NO!

Talking to God from the heart for a few minutes each morning is a great way to shift your focus from thinking that you're all alone—flying solo with a myriad of problems, challenges, and worries—to realizing that you're really just a co-pilot who can turn over the reins of power to a very loving, compassionate, and wise presence that has only your best interests in mind.

Here are some sample prayers to get you started:

Prayer for Faith in a Higher Power (Louise Hay)

In the infinity of life, where I am, all is perfect, whole, and complete. I believe in a power far greater than I am that flows through me every moment of every day. I open myself to the wisdom within, knowing that there is only One Intelligence in this Universe. Out of this One Intelligence comes all the answers, all the solutions, all the healings, and all the new creations. I trust this Power and Intelligence, knowing that whatever I need to know is revealed to me, and that whatever I need comes to me at the right time, space, and sequence. All is well in my world.

Prayer for Forgiving Another (Edemir Rossi)

Dear God,

There is someone who has hurt me deeply. I know that my ability to forgive this person is where my freedom lies, for my hatred and judgment are attacks upon myself. God, please help me. I surrender to You my thoughts of this person's guilt.

I know my unforgiving thoughts are hurting me, and yet I cannot seem to let them go. Dear Lord, I am willing to see this person's innocence and to understand the pain in him that would make him do such hurtful things to me. I am willing to forgive, but I need your strength to do so. I surrender this person to You. I surrender my pain to You. Heal him; heal me. Thank you.

Prayer for Forgiving Oneself (Kathleen Pasley)

Dear God,

I am finding it impossible to forgive myself. I have never felt lower in my life, and I cannot stop the negative self-talk in my head. Please help me to forgive myself because, right now, I am unable to do so. I am criticizing myself all the time. I am feeling guilty for so many things that I have done and the character flaws that I possess.

Please dissolve this hurt and pain. I am tired of beating myself up. Please show me how to love myself, as You do. Help me to value and forgive myself for my mistakes and shortcomings.

Sailor's Prayer

Dear God,

Please be good to me.

The sea is so wide,

and my boat is so small.

Prayer for Protection (Ernest Holmes)

The light of God surrounds me;

The love of God enfolds me;

The power of God protects me;

The presence of God watches over me;

Wherever I am, God is!

Prayer of St. Francis of Assisi

Lord, make me an instrument of Your peace!

Where there is hatred, let me sow love.

Where there is injury, pardon.

Where there is doubt, faith.

Where there is despair, hope.

Where there is darkness, light.

Where there is sadness, joy.

O Divine Master, grant that I may not so much seek

To be consoled as to console,

To be understood as to understand,

To be loved as to love.

For it is in giving that we receive,

It is in pardoning that we are pardoned,

It is in dying that we are born to eternal life.

The Serenity Prayer

God,

Grant me the serenity to accept the things I cannot change.

The courage to change the things I can.

And the wisdom to know the difference.

Mychal's Prayer (Father Mychal Judge, NY City Fire Department Chaplain, killed September 11, 2001)

Lord, take me where You want me to go.

Let me meet who you want me to meet.

Tell me what you want me to say.

And

Keep me out of your way.

The Easiest and Most Important Prayer of All

"HELP!!!"

The shortest prayer, often the most effective, is a single word with a few exclamation marks. This plea rallies the unseen spiritual world to your side and is open-ended enough to make the point that you don't really know what would help; you just know you need it! Asking for spiritual help works every time...maybe not in the way we expect or want, and often not in the time frame we'd like, but it will come.

Starting a Prayer Practice with a Friend

When I lived in Washington, D.C., I had a prayer partner for over fifteen years. Julie was my spiritual rock. She passed to the other side in 2018, and I miss her every day.

Julie and I would call each other every morning, no matter where we were. We both traveled a lot, but still never missed a day. Our ritual was to first read out loud something inspirational that always had a lesson in it. We often used a magazine called *The Science of Mind*, which features daily messages.

I'm a big fan of daily inspirational books, some of which you'll find listed in the Spiritual Literature section at the end of this book.

After reading the magazine's message for the day, Julie and I would each pray out loud, usually integrating the daily reading into our prayers. Each prayer usually ran from two to three minutes. It always started with gratitude for whatever we thought about that day. We would then each say our own prayer out loud and finally ask for help for ourselves or others who we knew were going through a difficult time.

Julie worked as the head concierge at the Washington, D.C. Four Seasons Hotel, just down the street from my house. If she was going to be working in the morning, she often stopped by, and we prayed before she had to leave—usually at 7 a.m. When she left, she would always say, "Have the best day of your life!" and I would always reply, "Onward and upward!" It was a terrific way to start the day.

Prayer for When You Don't Know What to Do

Many years ago, I was going through a very serious, bone-crunching depression. I was almost suicidal and felt that there was no way I was ever going to smile again. Catastrophizing about everything in my life and feeling overwhelmingly hopeless, I was lying on my couch in a catatonic state when I yelled to God, "HELP! I DON'T KNOW WHAT TO DO." By the next day, the darkness was lifting, and I started feeling like myself again. I know that my recovery was a direct result of my simple prayer to God.

Praying works. Take my word for it!

GUIDANCE

Always Listen to It

As I've said before, we are all on a spiritual journey—whether we realize it or not. Life is a winding path filled with clues and nudges, signs and synchronicities. Divine guidance is alive and well!

In my case, those Divine clues have sometimes been as clear as Hansel and Gretel's breadcrumbs…and I've still chosen to ignore them! Other times, I feel completely attuned—sensitized to inner guidance and open to the wisdom of the Divine—only to discover I've been having a one-way conversation with my ego all along.

One of the fundamental mistakes I can make, especially in my younger years, is listening to everyone else's input instead of my own inner wisdom.

As someone said,

> *My high school guidance counselor told me I'll always be useless.*
>
> *So, I became a guidance counselor.*

But I've come to believe this: If we accept that there's more to us than just our physical bodies and the material world around us… If we trust that we can be guided by a force wiser than our own... and if we remember to ask for a little Divine help along the way, we're far more likely to find ourselves floating downstream—rather than clawing and struggling upstream in the wrong direction.

The truth is, it's not about whether or not we're being guided—we are! The real question is: Are we noticing that guidance? And are we willing to listen? That takes practice. It also takes a mindset that's willing to let go of rigid expectations and surrender our attachment to how things should turn out.

As the saying goes:

I finally got a grip when I learned to let go.

or

We can make a plan, but we can't

plan the result.

I'd wager that nearly all of us have experienced at least two moments of unmistakable guidance: a sudden sense that saved us from a car crash, a quiet "tap on the shoulder" telling us to swerve, slow down, or speed up just in time. Or a moment of deep clarity or comfort during the loss of a loved one, when we felt something beyond ourselves holding us up.

And if you look back on your own life, I'm willing to bet you'll find other moments, too, times when there was no logical explanation for what you did, what happened, or why. But somehow... it felt like you were guided.

Loving My Special Trees

Whenever I've rented or bought a home, whether a condo, house, or apartment, I've always felt guided to the space that is perfect for me. Usually, it happens after looking at what feels like a million options. But once I step into the right place, I know almost immediately. There's a quiet certainty: This is it!

That's happened to me in Boston, Washington, D.C., and Naples, Florida. What I didn't realize, until my most recent move, was that the Universe seemed to have a consistent "bonus feature" in mind when guiding me to a place to live: a large, spectacular, and protective tree visible from inside the home. Now, that wouldn't be so unusual if I were a country girl, but being a city gal, jumbo trees aren't exactly easy to come by in urban settings!

Still, there was one outside my condo on Beacon Hill in Boston. It hung over my deck and was beautiful both in full bloom and with snow covering it.

In the Georgetown section of Washington, D.C., my 125-year-old townhouse had a living room with a massive picture window looking out at the largest cherry blossom tree in the city. It was stunning. When in bloom (only for a week), I was the most popular girl in town, with everyone I knew wanting to get a glimpse of Nature at its best! Sometimes, when I was by myself on a rainy summer night, I would sit in my garden under the canopy of the tree, staying completely dry, and listen to Maria Callas blasting on my stereo. Heaven!

I've always been drawn to city life, the energy, the political discussions, the culture, the food, the variety of people and the activities. Florida never even made the list as a possible place to retire. But when I started thinking about where I would go after leaving D.C., the name Naples, Florida, kept popping into my mind. I had only visited once and knew almost no one. (One dear friend lived there only in the winter.) Regardless, I've learned to pay close attention to these nudges, no matter how hairbrained they seem.

Naples, as it turns out, is a beautiful town on the Gulf that boasts a lovely downtown, lots of things going on, fabulous restaurants, art and culture, PLUS beautiful beaches and awesome sunsets.

My new home? A small, charming Floridian house with not one, not two, but three enormous banyan trees in the front yard. The trees look like something out of an illustrated fairy tale book. I didn't even know what a banyan tree was before moving here! And there the three of them were—majestic and awe inspiring, waiting for me to enjoy

Bingo! The Universe had done it again.

A Creative Idea Prompted by the Car Radio

Years ago, I was struggling with how to open a presentation on marketing and branding. I wanted something fresh, memorable, and a little unexpected, but I was totally blocked.

Then one day, while listening to NPR in the car, I heard an interviewee mention Betty Crocker, not a real person, of course, but a branding icon that's had eight different visual representations over the decades. The first one was a traditional older woman, another had a Jackie Kennedy-style bouffant, another was a businesswoman with a fake necktie (I always hated that look!), and even one that reflected the "yuppie" era. Half of them looked like they had never stepped foot in a kitchen, but all the outfits throughout the years were, of course, bright red.

It was ideal! The evolution of Betty Crocker became the perfect metaphor for brand identity shifting with the times, and my presentation wrote itself from there.

Receiving guidance doesn't mean you live in Candyland and expect the Universe to ping you with updates every five minutes (although, honestly, I'm beginning to think that might actually be possible, and one of my biggest goals in this lifetime!) But it does mean we learn not to rely solely on the rational mind.

Einstein said:

"I didn't arrive at my understanding of the fundamental laws of the Universe through my rational mind."

There are days when my brain feels like it has too many tabs open, and when that happens, I regress and don't see the clues. I rely too heavily on my "to-do" list, my phone calendar, and scattered thoughts to guide me. That's when I miss the magic.

Divine guidance doesn't usually arrive with trumpets and a celestial map. But if you stay open, you'll start to notice it in subtle, beautiful ways: a book falling off a shelf, a song on the radio, a phrase on a billboard, a passing comment from a stranger that lands exactly when you need it.

It's only when we let go of our plan and surrender to a greater one that we truly start to feel led by the Universe.

Experiencing Clear Guidance about My Dearest Friend

Think back to the times when you've lost someone you loved. Did you feel guided then? My most vivid experience of this came right before my closest friend, Julie, passed away six years ago. We had agreed that I'd visit her in the hospital after I returned from spending Christmas in Boston with my family.

The day before Christmas Eve, I was leaving on a 6 a.m. flight. A friend had borrowed my car, so there was nothing practical about my paying Julie a visit before the holiday. But something was nagging at me. I had a strong feeling I needed to deliver Julie's Christmas gift immediately, not to wait a few days as we had planned.

So, I followed the nudge. I took an Uber that evening and made the hour-long journey to the hospital. Thank God I did. That night, we laughed, we talked, we shared our unbreakable bond one last time. When I returned from New England, she had already slipped into a coma.

I was there for her passing, but we never spoke again. That night in the hospital, our last real moments together, was a gift I'll treasure forever. And I know in my soul, I was guided to make it happen.

Your intuition is always your biggest guidance, your soul speaking to you, your gut instinct, never, never, never ignore it! I'll leave the last word on this topic to Sylvester Stallone, of all people, who said:

"I think there comes a time in your life when you realize that

you need God in your life, God's word, and the

spiritual guidance that only He can give."

My thoughts EXACTLY!

MEDITATION AND MINDFULNESS

Practice, Practice, Practice

"Meditation needs to be demystified in Western culture. In many ways, meditation is no different than focusing your attention on anything else in this life. As a technique, we keep thinking we have to empty our minds of all thoughts or preoccupations. I have learned that for most of us in the Western world, this is virtually impossible."

- Edemir Rossi

Meditation allows the body to relax and to offset the effects of modern-day stress, both mentally and physically, to a much greater extent than any kind of passive relaxation or even strenuous exercise. While not necessarily "religious" in the traditional sense, meditation allows us to contact that peaceful, calm, rejuvenating, and infinitely creative place within our souls and within the silence of our "quiet minds."

If you have ever felt the contemplative relaxation of looking at a beautiful sunset, sat mesmerized at the ocean surf, or gazed endlessly into a burning fireplace...you already know the feeling.

Meditation is a wonderful technique for knowing who we are, what we are, and why we do the things we do. Meditation is an art form that requires discipline and perseverance. It is best to meditate in the morning before you start your day. Fifteen minutes will do; a half hour would be ideal.

If you do this faithfully, it is virtually impossible not to see a radical improvement in your daily life. There is no one right way to meditate. You might prefer guided meditations where someone speaks to you through a recording that helps you visualize and experience calming and relaxing scenes and thoughts, often with soothing background music.

There is an App on your iPhone called *Insight Timer*. They have scores of guided meditations on different topics, and I always find ones that I like. I recommend it highly.

Alternatively, you might want to recite a mantra or gaze at a candle to help quiet your mind. By simply putting yourself in a meditative posture and stating your intention to meditate, the spiritual world will rush in to help you. The mantra that feels right to me is: "Peace, Love" on the inbreath and "Harmony" on the outbreath. It's good to play around with words until you find the right mantra that resonates with you.

Many people feel they can't do meditation correctly and are concerned that they never seem to be able to quiet their minds. Don't even worry about this. Our attempts to steady, calm, or control our minds often merely stirs things up. Simply commit to a meditation practice, and you will be surprised at the results and your growing ability for your mind to naturally be at ease.

Meditation is different from relaxation. Of course, meditation will also bring you to a relaxed state. But its intention is different. Keep in mind that with meditation, we start to observe and to know ourselves. We start to feel an inner calm and happiness that doesn't depend on life's fortunes or misfortunes.

There are a few important basics that you want to be aware of as you progress in your meditation practice. When you meditate, always choose a comfortable position, either sitting on the floor or on a chair, remembering to keep your back straight. It is best to have both of your feet on the floor if you choose to sit in a chair. Don't lie down because, in this position, most of us naturally fall asleep, which is not the point of meditation.

Deep breathing is important for your meditation practice. The lungs are the "heart and soul" of our energetic system. Pay close attention to them because they stimulate, support, and give rhythm to your body. Our breathing is related to our emotions and thoughts. When thoughts and emotions are inharmonious, they will invariably cause breathing or respiratory problems.

The opposite is also true. By controlling your breathing, you can control your emotional and mental states. We cleanse and charge the overall human system through breathing.

Normal breathing uses only one-third of the capacity of our lungs. Prana is a high-frequency energy that is located in the air. When you use deep breathing techniques, you will triple the amount of prana you will bring into your system. Prana helps energize us and increase the effectiveness of our meditation.

The following instructions for a meditation practice are taken from the teachings of Herbert Benson, the doctor who first initiated training his patients in the power of the "Relaxation Response." With his approach, there are no spiritual overtones but just the desire to get into a meditative state of mind.

- Sit quietly in a comfortable position and close your eyes.

- Relax your muscles, beginning at the soles of your feet and slowly working up to your face. Keep them relaxed.

- Breathe in and out through your nose, becoming aware of the rhythm of your breathing. On the out breath, say the word "one" silently to yourself. You can also use the word "peace" or any other one syllable word that attracts you. Breathe in, breathe out, think "one"; breathe in, breathe out, think "one." Breathe easily and naturally.

- Continue for 10 to 20 minutes. You may open your eyes to check the time, but do not use an alarm. When you finish, sit quietly for several minutes, first with your eyes closed and later with your eyes open. Do not stand up for a few minutes.

- Don't worry about whether you are successful in achieving a deep level of relaxation. During the relaxation process, maintain a passive attitude and permit relaxation to occur at its own pace. When you notice your mind beginning to wander, gently refocus your attention on the mantra selected. Remain a neutral witness and watch your mind when it is involved in thoughts.

The more you practice, the more quickly you will enter a state of serenity and peace. Consider your meditation practice like a daily shower. It is not something that is an option, but a necessary part of your regular routine.

Mindfulness

Eckhart Tolle says:

"Realize deeply that the present moment is all you ever have.

Make the now the primary focus of your life."

The Buddha said:

"Do not dwell in the past, do not dream of the future,

Concentrate the mind on the present moment."

Mindfulness is the practice of being present and fully engaged in the current moment in daily life - aware of your thoughts, feelings, and surroundings without judgment. In contrast, meditation, while often similar in effect, is a formal practice or technique where you set aside time to focus your mind.

Mindfulness can be practiced anytime, anywhere – while eating, walking, talking, or working. Like meditation, it can reduce stress, enhance self-awareness, and deepen a spiritual connection. Here's an example of a mindful walking practice:

- Stand still for a moment. Feel the ground beneath your feet.

- Take a breath and bring your attention to your body.

- Walking slowly, with each step, notice the sensation of your feet lifting and touching the ground.

- Feel the movement in your legs, hips, and arms.

- Let your hands rest naturally or swing gently.

- What do you hear? Birds, traffic, wind?

- What do you see? Colors, shapes, light?

- What do you feel on your skin? Temperature, breeze, sun?

- If your mind wanders, gently say to yourself, "Just walking," and bring your attention back to the movement and sensations.

- When you're ready to stop, pause and take a deep breath.

- Notice how your body feels now compared with when you started.

Some of the benefits of practicing mindfulness are: increased mental clarity and focus; better emotional regulation such as managing stress, anxiety and depression; stronger physical health such as lowering blood pressure and strengthening the immune system; more self-awareness and insight; better relationships and communication such as increasing empathetic listening and compassion; and creating a sense of inner peace.

Start or Participate in a Meditation Group

When it comes to meditation, the rule is to "do as I say, not as I do." While I have a strong morning routine that focuses on spirit and lasts well over an hour, I am not the most faithful meditator in the world!

I was most faithful to a practice when I hosted a meditation group that was led by Edemir Rossi. We would meet as a group at my house every Wednesday night. Edemir would lead the evening, starting with a brief check-in, initiating a guided meditation, and then we would each meditate on our own until Edemir said we should come back into total consciousness. We then did a debrief with everyone sharing their experience.

Some of the meditators saw lights, sensed spiritual experiences, and had tremendous emotions that came up. I sat like a bump on a log when it came to sharing. I believe I was intimidated, but what I felt were the meditation skills of the other members of the group – never a good look! As the expression goes, in a group, you should "stay on your own mat" and not compare yourself to others in the room.

If you want to start your own group, here is the structure you might consider:

1. Welcome

    a. Brief check-in or reading

    b. Emphasize confidentiality and non-judgment

    c. Make sharing optional

2. Guided or silent meditation

    a.   Someone can guide it or play a recording

    b.   Close meditation after 30 to 40 minutes

3. Sharing and Discussion

    a.   Open floor for participants to reflect

    b.   Pose a question like: "What did you notice? or "How does this connect with daily life?"

4. Closing

    a.   Short reading or blessing

    b.   Share the next meeting details

Mindful Listening That Included a Peanut Butter Sandwich

A while back, I attended a three-day workshop at Omega – a lovely spiritual center in upstate New York. It was led by one of my favorite spiritual authors and teachers, Paul Ferrini.

Paul suggested we do a mindfulness exercise with a partner. We were asked first to pair up with someone. There was only one person in the room whom I *didn't* want to work with – a beautiful woman who was impeccably dressed and looked like she had "life by the tail"...a regular "I have it all" kind of a person who didn't have a care in the world.

Guess who made a beeline for me? The Beauty Queen! Natch! We sat down in two chairs opposite each other. The instruction was to answer a question: "What is a word that defined your last week and why?" One person was to share without being interrupted. The other person was to listen mindfully by focusing entirely on the speaker; not giving advice, no nodding, or shaking their head; and not planning what to say next. The other person was to share what the speaker's comments brought up for them and why.

I started and used "Conflict" as my word and told her about a serious problem I was having with a work colleague who was also a friend, and I didn't know what to do about it without losing the friendship. Pretty boring!

When the Beauty Queen had to respond by not commiserating, not offering a solution but telling me what my story had reminded her of, her word was "Peanut Butter Sandwich" and she went on to say she suffered with an eating disorder, felt it was ruining her marriage and making her a poor parent with an autistic child. As you can imagine, I almost fell off my chair. Another lesson in not jumping to conclusions by appearances! We made another round of this unconditional listening, but I honestly don't remember what that was about.

After we had both shared twice, we were to speak slowly and kindly to our partner, without trying to fix, solve, or impress, and then thank the person for listening. Do you know how hard it is not to offer advice, express sympathy, or respond at all to another person's problem? But it does make you aware of how often we're not totally listening with undivided attention to another person talking...we're too busy thinking about what we are going to say next!

I'll never forget the experience! It's a wonderful exercise to do with a partner, anyone with whom you would like to improve communication with. Try mindful listening and you'll be changed forever.

AUTHENTICITY

Being Real

John Lennon said:

"Being honest may not get you many friends

But it will always get you the right ones."

William Shakespeare wrote:

"To thine own self be true."

If there's one thing to aspire to on a spiritual path, it's being authentic – true to yourself AND willing to be that to the outside world. A tall order! I honestly believe that, as someone said: Be yourself. Authenticity trumps cool every time!

I try to be self-aware, which invariably requires looking inside myself the way I TRULY am. I've certainly done enough therapy to get the basic gist of who I am with the blinders off.

And, being a student of spirituality, I KNOW that happiness is an inside job and that you must be willing to let a lot of "stuff" go before the real you emerges. As a spiritual practice, authenticity calls for us to live in alignment with our true selves. Beyond our masks, roles, or societal expectations, we can honor our inner truth, listen to our soul's voice, and act in ways that reflect our deepest values and beliefs. The more we have on the inside, the less we need on the outside. I only want one thing from fake people: DISTANCE.

Bryant McGill writes:

"So many people cover-up things within themselves. They smile when they really need to frown. They 'laugh' nervously when they are uneasy and uncomfortable. They try to make it 'all right' so everything can be 'perfect' and 'fine.' We fake perfect, so others don't have to experience any unpleasant realities."

But…am I always the real me? Not afraid to be myself? Not looking outside for reinforcement? Happy with what I see in the mirror? Courageous enough to be imperfect and vulnerable? Knowing that I'm always being honest with myself and others? Feeling like I always respond in a way that suits who I am? Never hide a part of myself? You've got to be kidding. No question about it, I don't fit the bill every time…I'm far from perfect about being authentic and still have a looooong way to go!

On the other hand, I honestly believe that when it comes to authenticity, I do better than most. I've dropped my preoccupation with what others think and do not try to be someone I'm not. What you see is what you get. I have learned to be myself, trust myself, and express myself.

Diana Ross said:

"I can be a better me than anyone can."

That's true of each of us. Let's vow to remember it!

I Loved Dr. Kildare BUT...

I was in middle school – probably 5th or 6th grade. I had a major crush on an actor who played Dr. Kildare on a show that was on TV every Thursday night. While other kids in my class were swooning and talking about Richard Chamberlain, who played Dr. Kildare, I pretended I didn't really care. I thought it was silly to express such an absurd attraction, even though I felt it myself. But I certainly did NOT want to admit it.

One Thursday, one of the girls came in with a knock-off white doctor's shirt on, complete with the appropriate collar and buttons at the top. By the following week, half the girls were wearing the same shirt, and by the third week, all the girls were wearing the shirt on every Thursday – except for me, of course.

I wanted to stick to my guns, so I became the odd man out on a weekly basis. Did I care? Yes, of course. But the minute I made a stand, I was determined to continue it. Was I self-conscious about it? You bet! Looking back on it, I am pleased that as a young girl I had the authenticity not to wear that shirt. On the other hand, I would have been much more comfortable with the girls in my class if I had gone along with the masses. Sometimes being authentic has its price to pay!

Open Mouth...Insert Foot

There were times when my determination to be authentic backfired. Like the time I was in college and got into the dormitory elevator with a blind student who was sharing the ride with me. Marianne was in my

English class, so I said: "If you haven't *seen* me, you must have heard me!"

Foot in mouth disease! She seemed ok regardless of my faux pas, and we talked every day before class after that incident. I always liked to think that she was pleased that someone called her condition out and didn't dance around it. Could be wishful thinking!

A Wonderful Experience with B.F. Skinner

While I was in the throes of my business career in Boston, I was invited to a wonderful event that included all the people from New England who had ever been on the cover of *Time Magazine*. The celebrities included everyone from Buckminster Fuller to John Updike; from Julia Child to Teddy Kennedy.

Not one to be shy, during the cocktail reception, I managed to meet all of the luminaries I really admired. Each of the honorees sat at a different table, a great way to get them to mingle and to please the guests at the same time. My place card had B.F. Skinner's name on the back of it because my date and I would be sitting at his table. The minute Skinner sat down, I made a beeline to sit next to him before anyone else got to the table.

B.F. Skinner was a famed behavior psychologist. He believed that people's and animals' behavior is shaped by rewards and punishments. He proved that if you reward a behavior, it's more likely to happen again, and if you punish it or ignore it, it's less likely to happen. He invented a device called the "Skinner Box" to study how animals learn through this system. In psychological circles, Skinner was a BIG deal, and since I was interested in his work, I was really excited to meet him.

As we were introducing ourselves, for some crazy reason, I said the first thing that came into my head. Since he seemed to be by himself, I asked him, "Is your wife dead?" He said, "No, she's sitting right across the table!"

My date that night never let me live it down, but this is the kind of authentic (or is it obnoxious?!) me that can come out. Faux pas that it was, I had one of the most interesting conversations of my life, talking to this incredible man who had such an influence on the field of psychology. Also, I felt like all our defenses were down, and we both, in that brief time together, expressed our authentic selves and really liked each other.

Skinner was in his 80s; I was in my early 30s, but we really had a "soul connection." He was teaching at Harvard at the time and invited me to his office, but I thought better of it.

These three examples show how "out there" I can be. I used to be embarrassed about these kinds of experiences, but you know what? Now I say that these brief encounters epitomize the uniqueness of me. Not always tactful but speaking from the heart.

You know what I think is true? It came up when I started researching the topic of authenticity. I read the following anonymous quote:

"Finding yourself is really not the way it works. You aren't a ten-dollar bill in last winter's coat pocket. You are also not lost. Your true self is right there, buried under cultural conditioning, other people's opinions, and inaccurate

conclusions you drew as a kid that became your beliefs about who you are. 'Finding Yourself' is actually returning to yourself. An unlearning, an excavation, a remembering of who you were before the world got its hands on you."

Let's face it, you know the authentic you better than anyone else!

In fact, as someone said:

Nobody knows the absolute truth, except for cats, and

they're pretty tight-lipped about it.

Most important of all, Dr. Seuss sums this up perfectly:

Today you are you,

That is truer than true.

There is no one alive

Who is Youer than You!

Thank God for that!

KINDNESS AND EMPATHY

A Higher Intelligence

There is no greater intelligence than kindness. There is no greater emotion than empathy.

Sure, most of the time, we can be kind and empathetic to those we love and cherish. But when it comes to the rest of the world, we find it a bit more of a challenge. When dealing with cranky, rude, unpleasant, narcissistic, or mean people, our kindness and empathy inclinations can quickly and easily dissipate. In fact,

Some people just need a high-five.

In the face. With a chair.

Henry Wadsworth Longfellow pointed out:

If we could read the secret history of our enemies, we should

find in each one's life sorrow and suffering enough

to disarm all our hostility.

It's all well and good under many circumstances to show gentle kindness and heartfelt empathy. But I believe many of us have a hard time when we interact with people we don't like or whose political leanings clash with ours.

I don't know about you, but I'm finding that the kindest thing I can do for myself and for the person whose views diametrically oppose mine is to shut up and avoid the conversation altogether. In other words, wimp out completely when it comes to having a civilized discussion on the topic. I hate to admit it, but I think I've come to understand my limits at this point in my "Earth School assignments." A friendly chat about my opinions with someone who passionately disagrees with me can feel far out of reach.

There was a time when I welcomed a good debate about American politics, national and international news, and even juicy Washington gossip. What's it like now? The other day, I found myself begging a friend who, in fact, thinks the same way I do, that we avoid politics entirely.

Why? Because my blood starts boiling and my heart starts racing when I even watch the news, much less talk to people about it. I admit it, I'm in a complete conundrum about how to handle these strong emotions and, yes, sometimes murderous thoughts.

It's painful to watch the news these days, Fox or CNN; Laura Ingraham or Rachel Maddow; Sean Hannity or Anderson Cooper. Their views make perfect sense to completely different audiences, each of which takes them as gospel truth.

I keep asking myself: Is there a spiritual way to deal with this? I've only come up with one. Empathy—and realistically, that's mighty hard to show.

Henry David Thoreau said of empathy:

"Could a greater miracle take place than for us to look through

each other's eyes for an instant?"

I honestly believe that love is the lynchpin of our human experience, and fear is the emotion that can derail us every time. So, what to do? When we're about to be unkind, a good alternative message comes from Buddhist monk, Pema Chödrön, who quotes her teacher, Trungpa Rinpoche, as saying:

You should never have expectations for other people.

Just be kind to them.

His message is that setting goals for others is asking them to live up to our own ideals. Instead, we should always express kindness. That can be a tall order when nerves are frazzled and expectations—our own and others'—are high.

Elizabeth Kübler-Ross, the renowned doctor who specialized in death and dying, once wrote:

"I have never met a person whose greatest need was anything other than real, unconditional love. You find it in a simple act of kindness toward someone

who needs help. There is no mistaking love."

Kindness is a trait we should strive to develop every day and every minute of our lives. It is one of the primary pillars of living a worthwhile and spiritual life.

Henry James said it beautifully:

Three things in human life are important.

The first is to be kind.

The second is to be kind.

The third is to be kind."

Here are some rules for those of us who are determined to express kindness:

- Have compassion for, and show kindness to, ourselves as well as others.
- Do not engage in arguments, shouting matches, or snarky emails and Facebook posts with those who think differently than we do.
- Vow not to lose important relationships in our lives because of our differences.
- Be empathetic toward everyone else who is experiencing the same high anxiety that you are—and right now, that's just about everyone in the country.

If we can't see eye to eye, let's try heart to heart!

Extending Kindness to Strangers

Years ago, when I was constantly traveling on business, one day I was sitting in the frequent flyers' lounge for Delta Airlines. I started talking to this friendly guy whose travel schedule made my frequent times waiting at airports look like a cakewalk.

He said to me that through all his travels, he had learned one simple thing: the magic of kindness with service people. Whether it was with a waiter, a cabbie, a skycap, a redcap, a shoeshine person, a concierge, or a maître d', he would always give them approximately 20% more than they would expect as a good tip. In other words, he was always a little kinder than necessary.

His rationale was that whatever extra cash came out of his pocket, when added up at the end of the year, didn't really amount to that much. But that kind of generosity could really make the recipient's day and restore their faith in humanity. If you have the power to make someone happy, DO IT. The world needs more of that.

As someone once said,

"Be the person your dog knows you to be."

Kindness is more than deeds. It goes much further than just being nice. It is an attitude, an expression, a look, or a touch. It is anything that lifts another person. Kindness is seeing the best in others when they can't see it themselves. A kind person considers the feelings of others, tries to help them, and avoids actions that do harm.

I am no longer impressed by wealth, social status, or job title. I am impressed by the way someone treats other human beings.

Buddha said:

"Life is so very difficult. How can we be anything but kind?"

It is all too easy to underestimate the power of a touch, a smile, a kind word, a listening ear, a nod of encouragement, an honest compliment, an unexpected deed, or the smallest act of caring—all of which have the potential to improve a mood, soothe a hurt, or even turn a life around.

"A little less judgment; a lot more kindness" is a formula to remember at all times. It has been said:

"Everyone is fighting a battle you know nothing about."

and

"So many people are hanging by the thinnest thread. Treat people well.

You could just be that thread."

Let's put kindness back into humankind. During these times of rude behavior, unkind insults, hurtful humor, and unrelenting partisanship, let's turn to kindness.

As Maya Angelou said:

"Try to be a rainbow in someone else's cloud."

Helping Someone in Distress

My brother Richard can be quiet and reflective, so when he speaks, you listen. He was the older of my two brothers when my father died – he was only 4 years old! My mother thoughtlessly placed him at the head of our dining room table once my father was no longer with us. Quite the responsibility for someone barely out of the toddler stage!

So, my brother had an early leadership role in the family that, for me, has stuck through adulthood even though he's my junior by nine years. Often, when I have a problem, Richard is my "go to" problem solver.

It was Easter Day when I was still living in Boston; Richard and I were on my back deck. Back in those days, I suffered a great deal with depression. This particular holiday, I was VERY depressed, feeling hopeless, helpless, fearful, and alone. Believe me, I wasn't even good for a smile on that holiday. No chocolate bunny was going to transform me into a happy person! I was taking medications but for some reason they weren't working (which was rare for me and made me even more discouraged.)

Stevie Ray Vaughan said:

"The way people come into your life when you need them, it's wonderful,

and it happens in so many ways. It's like having an angel.

Somebody comes along and helps you get right."

That was certainly the case on that Easter Sunday! Richard and I were making small talk on a beautiful sunny day, but I was hardly keeping up with the simplest things we discussed. In my darkest hours, he always knows how to come up with perfect solutions – usually very simple and matter of fact. His sensibility is such that he can be counted on to come through with the right words to say at the right time.

He had once been in a very deep depression himself, so he was able to speak to me with first-hand knowledge on the matter. He also knew better than to try to cheer me up because that wasn't going to do the trick. My mood was WAY beyond THAT solution.

Richard assured me that I would slowly and surely get better…the best advice and kindness I could receive. He continued to tell me that during his darkest time, he woke up one day and felt slightly better. Not a lot, but enough to keep him hanging on. Once the depression started moving away from him, he saw and experienced that there was nothing final about a depressive episode, and with time and incremental improvements every day, he felt back to normal within a month.

A friend, who also experienced severe depression in her life, mentioned that depression can be described in one word: hopelessness. Unbeknownst to him, Richard gave me the perfect message of hope just when I needed it. He didn't realize it at the time, but I was having suicidal thoughts, so he virtually saved my life. Thank you, Rich.

Show Kindness and Empathy to Yourself

Most of the time that I lived in Boston, I lived in a five-story townhouse on Beacon Hill. These houses were so old that they still had the characteristics of a home from the early 19th century. The first floor would have been the kitchen; the second floor, the living room; and the bedrooms were on the remaining floors.

I was fortunate enough to live on the second floor, which would have been the parlor, with very high ceilings and tall windows. There were two fireplaces. The floors were all wooden. There was one bedroom, a small office, one bathroom, and a deck in the back. The first three years I lived there, I was a renter. Everyone else owned theirs. (I did eventually purchase the unit.)

My downstairs neighbor was a bit of a weirdo—nobody ever visited Nancy, and you never heard a TV or a stereo playing. In fact, the whole first floor felt rather dead. She was one of those people who stared out the window to make sure no one was going to break in or do something she didn't approve of, which was just about everything.

One morning, Nancy, ever vigilant about the "comings and goings" in the building, caught me leaving on my way to work. She very nicely asked me to attend the building's condo meeting that evening. Since I was the only renter, I thought that was a thoughtful invitation for her to extend.

The minute I walked into her living room, she handed me a glass of wine and introduced me to the neighbors I had never met before. Then Nancy said, "This meeting is about you!" I almost fainted. What???

She proceeded to tell me that there was too much activity in my unit (I had the nerve to throw a party), and that my music was too loud. My shoes were too loud (I was always wearing heels when I came home from work), and she objected to my walking around on the wooden floors. That I could understand. But when she said she couldn't stand hearing the sound of my voice when I was on my deck, that was the straw that broke the camel's back. I never spoke to Nancy again, as my number one critic and the instigator of that ambush!

Let's not forget that we need to be kind to ourselves as well as to everyone else. Years later, I ran into Nancy in a store and just turned away without saying hello. Not my style, but I guess I just couldn't let that glass of wine "set-up" completely go. Maybe I need to practice one of my forgiveness exercises on Nancy. I honestly think, in this little story, I was protecting my boundaries—and that's always a kind thing towards ourselves.

BE A BRIGHT LIGHT

Each of Us Can Be One

I can't think of a better compliment to give someone than that he or she is a Bright Light. For me, bonafide Bright Lights are few and far between; sometimes we recognize them right off the bat, other times it takes a while, or experiencing a tough time in your life to recognize these special people.

A person who is a Bright Light in this world can be anyone – in fact, it could and should be everyone! The magic formula is to be our authentic selves and to have a strong desire to help and to be an uplifting presence for others. On the other hand, some of the brightest lights are those who don't even know that this is what they are. They don't need to be loud or famous. Often, it's their quiet consistency, warmth, and wisdom that leaves the deepest impact.

Here are some other characteristics that tend to be seen in Bright Lights. They are:

- Kind and compassionate – they genuinely care for others and show empathy in both big and small ways.

- Authentic – they live in alignment with their truth and values, inspiring others to do the same.
- Encouraging – they see potential in people and remind them of their worth, especially when they forget it themselves.
- Joyful and Peaceful – they know life can't be perfect, but they still know how to generate good feelings; they have cultivated inner strength and grace.
- Hopeful – they carry light into dark places, offering perspective, laughter, or simply their presence when it's needed most.
- Grounded in love – even when it's difficult.

It's been said:

"You can recognize a saint by his utter ordinariness as well as extraordinary kindness, presence, and generosity."

The same thing could be said for a true Bright Light. Another frequent characteristic of a Bright Light is that they can view everyone with love and compassion. Jerry Jampolsky, author of *Love is Letting Go of Fear*, put it this way:

"They can look at a person's light, not their lampshade."

William Wordsworth said:

"The best portion of a good man's life is his little, nameless, unremembered acts of kindness and of love."

So, how can the rest of us let our light shine and help others who are fighting their own battles?

TEN EASY WAYS TO LET YOUR LIGHT SHINE

1. Don't forget to smile.
2. Be there for a friend, family member, or work colleague.
3. Give genuine compliments.
4. Be friendly (even to strangers).
5. Share your optimism and gratitude.
6. Listen with intent.
7. Empathize with others.
8. Laugh or cause laughter freely.
9. Find the good in everyone who crosses your path.
10. Be your authentic self.

ANY time is a particularly good time to shine your own light and recognize the light in others.

Wayne Dyer wrote:

> *"See the light in others and treat them as*
>
> *if that's all you see."*

Nelson Mandela said:

> *"It never hurts to see the good in someone;*
>
> *they often act better for it."*

Oprah Winfrey claims:

> *"You have to find out what sparks a light in you,*
>
> *so that you, in your own way, can*
>
> *illuminate the world."*

Bright Lights Help Us Get Through Tough Times

I was thirteen years old when I had my first encounter with a Bright Light. My father, at the age of 47, was fatally sick with cancer. Right after he was diagnosed, my youngest brother was born. The timing was very difficult in some ways, but Peter was such a blessing in our lives that we were somehow able to gut through the next 14 months before my father died.

In no small part, Peter was the shining Bright Light that we all needed at that time. We were all involved with taking care of him, except for my other brother, who was only four years old at the time (another blessing in our lives!) There is nothing like a baby to be a great distraction.

Martin Luther King, Jr. so wisely said:

"Out of the mountain of despair, a stone of hope."

Peter was a special kid who was happy and buoyant. We were all so preoccupied with my father's illness, I'm afraid Peter was often left to fend for himself. We would put him in his playpen, and he'd always make us laugh with his antics and joyful nature. Just what the doctor ordered during such a heartbreaking time!

When Peter was old enough to climb out of his crib (which was no easy task!), he liked to figure out how to get his bedroom door open. We had a landing that looked out over our living room. Whenever he made his escape from his room, one of us would promptly go upstairs and put him back in his crib. One time, Peter was so determined to spread his wings that he came out of his room with a small wastepaper basket over his head. He was confident that if he couldn't see us, we wouldn't be able to see him! It was hysterical!

I honestly believe that this little brother of mine was a gift from God. A good piece of wisdom I received from this experience was: When your light shines bright, others can see their way out of the darkness.

Bright Lights Can Be Placed in Unlikely Environments

Another incredibly Bright Light was Julie Saunders, who I have spoken about frequently. It broke my heart when she passed away at the young age of 59. She had a smile that lit up every room, an inner glow that was palpable. She was the head concierge at the Washington Four Seasons Hotel, a very high-pressure job, and was even able to charm and honor the many difficult and often snooty customers she had to deal with there.

One might not suspect that the role of a concierge in a ritzy hotel would be where God chose to place such a powerful Lightworker. In time, I came to believe that some of these rich and often belligerent, sometimes soulless people needed to see Julie in action to "get it" for themselves. She was a "Concierge of the Spirit" and lived by the saying: Work is love made visible.

She viewed every person she encountered as an opportunity to serve and grow spiritually. I'm sure there were many times when she smiled through gritted teeth.

Hugh Prather wrote:

"Spiritual damage control is acting with kindness

when you don't want to."

Julie virtually gave off a light…she was very spiritual and knew how to walk the walk and talk the talk. She was hardly a saint and, like all of us, had her bad days. But everyone loved her, and she reciprocated in kind.

Julie's death was gut-wrenching for me - the second worst tragedy I have ever lived through. She was so beloved that close to 500 people, all fans, came to her memorial service.

Julie's favorite parting line when leaving your presence was:

"Have the best day of your life!"

She meant it and lived by it herself. When I was grouchy or depressed, I would cringe when she said those words. It took me a lot of spiritual work to recognize that this is actually possible!

There are some who bring light so great in the world that even after they have gone, their bright light remains. Julie was one of those people!

Bright Lights Can Make Us Laugh

How many difficult aspects of life can be foisted upon us? The list is endless. Like facing a scary diagnosis for yourself or someone you love; dealing with physical or emotional pain; being riddled with anxiety; feeling depressed; grieving over the loss of a loved one; getting fired or rejected in any way; doing poorly on a test, an interview or a performance; getting a divorce; being disappointed in yourself or someone else. Have I forgotten anything?!

Eventually, if not immediately, laughter is always the perfect antidote! Not that laughing is something we can always do, at least not in the middle or right after the difficulty or the heartache is staring at us in the face. BUT we'll feel a WHOLE lot better once the giggling and guffawing can begin again.

If there is a better way than laughter to circumvent those miserable feelings when you're having a bad day - a minor league or even a major one – I'd like to hear about it!

I come from a large Irish family with over 30 cousins, where laughter and humor are a major part of the soul; in fact, a good side-splitting, unabashed laugh is just about the solution to everything.

Audrey Hepburn said:

"I like people who make me laugh.

I honestly think that laughing is the

thing I like most. It cures a multitude

of ills. It's probably the most important

thing in a person."

I have a girlfriend from college who is full of life and laughter, always a Bright Light to everyone who knows her. Her name is Anne Austin, her nickname is Easter (her maiden name was East.)

Easter is one of the funniest people you could ever meet. She is adept at the sarcastic quip, the friendly put down or the perfect self-deprecating remark. I love all of it, and whenever I need a lift, I pick up the phone and talk to Easter. Her presence in person or through a phone line always has me rolling on the ground laughing – she is the perfect mood enhancer!

It's been said: laughter is the shock absorber that eases the blows of life. Another one I can relate to is: laughter is the shortest distance between two people.

Easter collects costumes – and not the CVS kind. Many are custom-made for her and include wigs or hats, and shoes to match. She has costumes for: Tina Turner, Cher, Queen Elizabeth, Beetlejuice, the Mad Hatter, Michael Jackson, John Travolta, Elvis Presley, George Washington, Alice in Wonderland, and an Abba singer, to name a few. In fact, Easter has close to 50 costumes, each one of them accompanied by a skit. You'd have to see one of them to believe it!

One time, a group of friends and Easter flew to Las Vegas. She was dressed as Elvis and then had the nerve to get up and sing "You Ain't Nothin' But A Hound Dog" in front of the entire plane!

I was able to see her do her Tina Turner impersonation to the song, "Proud Mary", complete with a very short, gold fringe dress and high-heeled shoes. Her costume for John Travolta included a white suit and shirt, black patent leather shoes, a gold necklace around her neck, and even fake hair on her chest!

Buddha said:

"There is no path to happiness. Happiness is the path."

You don't have to tell Easter that…she's already living her life to represent this.

I'm sure you also have people in your life who are Bright Lights. A lot of times, Bright Lights don't know this for themselves. So, be sure to thank them for the joy that they have brought to you and many others.

Don't forget…

YOU, too, can be a bright light.

So go out there and shine!

SPIRITUAL LITERATURE

"There's no point at which we've learned everything we ever need to know, become as healthy as we ever need to be, or done every good thing we could possibly do."

\- Eric Harvey

Most of us have a great deal of catching up to do when it comes to spiritual knowledge. It's a rare formal learning setting where the topic of God, a Higher Power or the Divine is even discussed, much less taught. The unexpected benefits of reading about spirituality is that it is fun and mind expanding to launch into the study of such a fascinating and compelling topic that has application in everyday life.

Even for those who were brought up in a religiously oriented home, spiritual study can be an eye-opening experience. Spirituality and its associated literature are quite different from organized religion. Spirituality is very personal, experiential and connects us to a wider world view, beyond our bodies and minds. It offers no specific roadmap to follow but allows us to find the divinity, the soul, the heart within our own being.

When you read a spiritual book, enjoy the parts that resonate with you and ignore the rest. Some concepts may sound too "far out" or untrue for you. But also, remember, something that sounds too weird or strange to you today might make perfect sense to you in a few years.

Buddhism might appeal to you now but *A Course in Miracles* might be a good fit down the road. The advantage we have today is that there are so many choices as we move towards a universal understanding that all religions and spiritual studies lead in the same direction and towards the same goal of a closer relationship with God.

Books that are starred (**) are those that I recommend most highly.

A Course in Miracles (ACIM) and Related Books

A Course in Miracles (ACIM), The Foundation for Inner Peace

ACIM is the backbone of my spiritual studies. *The Course* is a self-study curriculum that helps you to view life in a totally new way, leading to inner peace and happiness. It can be a daunting undertaking but well worth the effort. There is a Text which describes ACIM principles; a Workbook for Students, which consists of 365 lessons, an exercise for each day of the year; and a Manual for Teachers which helps students practice the messages found in the Course. You will find profound truth on every page.

A Return to Love, Marianne Williamson

Marianne Williamson is the best translator and teacher of ACIM. Her book, a number one best seller, is beautifully written and provides in easy-to-understand terms, the essence of the Course and how to apply it in your life. A wonderful read.

The Course in Miracles Experiment, Pam Grout

A Year of Miracles (daily readings), Marianne Williamson

Holy Shifts (daily readings), Robert Holden, PhD

Love is Letting Go of Fear, Gerald Jampolsky

The Universe Has Your Back, Gabrielle Bernstein

52 Ways to Live the Course in Miracles, Karen Casey

A compact rendition of how to live with love and forgiveness at the center of your life. Contains 52 positive affirmations and meditations to find inner peace. Concise and easy to understand.

A Course in Miracles Made Easy, Alan Cohen

Living A Course in Miracles, John Mundy

A Course in Miracles Clarified, Raymond Wells

A Course in Miracles: The Direct Path, D. McCauley

Daily Readings – Perfect for Reading Every Morning

A Daily Dose of Sanity: A Five-Minute Soul Recharge for Every Day of the Year, Alan Cohen

In a uniquely warm and down-to-earth way, Cohen presents, for each day-of-the-year, a theme, a quotation, a true-to-life anecdote, a short lesson, a question for self-study and an empowering affirmation.

A Deep Breath of Life: Daily Inspiration for Heart-Centered Living, Alan Cohen
**

Each day's message includes a theme, a quote of wisdom, a parable or real-life anecdote, a prayer and an affirmation. In just a few minutes every day, you can step back from your worldly activity and draw in a deep breath of spiritual lessons and renewal.

Each Day a New Beginning, Karen Casey

Opening Doors Within, Eileen Caddy

Trust Life: Love Yourself Every Day with Wisdom, Louise Hay

Since Louise's writing was my first introduction to a spiritual life, anything that she writes gets my vote. As a founder of the self-help movement, she knows how to guide you to the truth of who you are: powerful, loving and lovable. A great way to start out each day.

Daily Reflections from Dr. David Hawkins, David Hawkins

Everyday Wisdom, Wayne Dyer

365 of Science of Mind, Ernest Holmes

Everyday Spirit, Mary Davis

Prayers

Illuminata: A Return to Prayer, Marianne Williamson

This is my favorite prayer book. It provides prayers to use for every topic from mending broken relationships to recognizing that work is another way you can engage in spiritual practice. A beautiful resource, it can introduce prayer into your life in a practical and engaging way.

Intimate Conversations with the Divine, Carolyn Myss

The Energy of Prayer, Thich Nhat Kahn

My Favorite Spiritual Authors Listed with Their Books

Karen Casey

Let Go Now: Embrace Detachment as a Path to Freedom **

I love Karen Casey's writing. This book is about setting healthy boundaries and helps the reader move from taking care of others and toward taking care of ourselves. Her books are very accessible, easy to read and inspirational. In 200 short lessons, she illustrates how removing co-dependency from our lives leads to a life of balance and freedom.

The Long Good Life

Change Your Mind and Your Life Will Follow

Deepak Chopra

The Seven Spiritual Laws of Success

Twenty Spiritual Lessons for Creating the Life You Want

Alan Cohen

The Grace Factor

The Tao Made Easy

The Master Keys of Healing

Soul and Destiny

Wayne Dyer

Change Your Thoughts – Change Your Life

There's a Spiritual Solution to Every Problem: The Power of Love, Harmony, and Service **

Any book you pick up from Wayne Dyer is a pleasure to read and contains great wisdom. This one is my favorite of his, but I would recommend you might want to read *Change Your Thoughts – Change Your Life* or *The Power of Intention* first. Wayne, with his trademark wit and wisdom, offers compelling testimony on the idea that there is an omnipotent presence. There is always a spiritual force at our fingertips that contains the solution to your problems.

The Power of Intention

Wishes Fulfilled

Living the Wisdom of the Tao

Excuses Begone!

Manifest Your Destiny

Paul Ferrini

Healing Your Life

Love Without Conditions: Reflections of the Christ Mind

David Hawkins

In the World but Not of It

The Path to Spiritual Advancement

The Ego is Not the Real You

Thich Nhat Hahn

Happiness

The Art of Living

Louise Hay

You Can Heal Your Life **

My all-time favorite spiritual book. Louise was my first introduction to spirituality and this book is where I often suggest people start their studies. It has sold over 50 million copies! Always relatable with simple, straightforward and powerful advice about how our thoughts create our reality. The best introduction to the power of affirmations you could ever read.

Power Thoughts

Life Loves You, Louise Hay and Robert Holden

Heart Thoughts

The Power is Within You

Gina Lake

A Heroic Life

Angels, Masters and Guides

The Jesus Trilogy

Cycles of the Soul

Radiance: Experiencing Divine Presence

The Shift: Becoming Your Best Self **

Clearly, from the shear number of books I list here of Gina Lake's, her work resonates with me. I recommend everything she has written but suggest you get your feet wet with some of the above suggestions before tackling her more recent work. This book tells how when you change your thoughts, your life changes profoundly.

From Stress to Stillness: Tools for Inner Peace

Every Flower Fades: Embracing Aging and Change

Love and Surrender: New Teachings from Jesus

What Jesus Wants You to Know Today

All Grace

Jamie Kern Lima

*Believe It: How to Go from Underestimated to Unstoppable **

Jamie has such an impressive and heartfelt life story and success. Her message is always practical and empowering, especially for women. She urges the reader to know you have what it takes, to believe in yourself and go from doubting yourself to knowing you're enough. Jamie takes you on her personal journey with vulnerability and honesty, of how she turned a company from a mere idea to one she sold to L'Oreal for over a billion dollars.

Worthy

Hugh Prather

How to Live in the World and Still Be Happy

Note to Myself

Don Miguel Ruiz

The Four Agreements

The Fifth Agreement

Living a Life of Awareness

Eckhart Tolle

Stillness Speaks

The Power of Now

Essays

The Pivot Year, Brianna Wiest

101 Essays That Will Change Your Life, Brianna Wiest

Simple Reminders, Bryant McGill **

This is a Wall Street Journal and USA Today Best Seller. Teaches the tools and patterns of thinking to cultivate more beauty in life, build confidence, escape from toxic relationships, move through pain and conflict, forgive people who have hurt you and uncover your highest purpose in life.

Other Miscellaneous Recommendations

After the Ecstasy, the Laundry: How the Heart Grows Wise on the Spiritual Path, Jack Kornfield

Archangels and Ascended Masters, Doreen Virtue, Ph.D.

The Light Worker's Way, Doreen Virtue, Ph.D.

Attitudes of Gratitude, M.J. Ryan

Ask and It Is Given, Jerry Hicks and Esther Hicks

The Power of Karma, Mary T. Brown

Repetition: Past Lives, Life and Rebirth, Doris Eliana Cohen, Ph.D.

Return of the Children of Light, Judith Bluestone Polich

Row, Row, Row Your Boat: A Guide for Living Life in the Divine Flow, Steven Lane Taylor

This Thing Called You, Ernest Holmes

Warrior of the Light, Paulo Coelho

Wherever You Go, There You Are, Jon Kabbot-Zinn

SPIRITUAL AND SOOTHING MUSIC

Finally, I have included favorite spiritual and relaxing music that can be used for meditation or simply to enjoy some soothing vibes with a glass of wine in front of a fireplace. All the music can be accessed on Spotify, which is what I use for my own listening.

Albums

African

Songs of Life by African Voices

Native American

Carlos Nakai

Songs of the Morning Star

Inner Voice

Matriarch: Iroquois Women's Songs by Joanne Shenandoah

Chants

Deva Premal

The Essence

Into Silence

Dakashina

Love Is Space

Krishna Das

Heart Full of Soul

Breath of the Heart

Pilgrim Heart

Live on Earth…For a Limited Time Only

Rain of Blessings by Lama Gyurme and Jean Philippe Rykiel

Beyond by Tina Turner

Gregorian Chants by Monks of the Abbey of Notre Dame

Harp Music

Hilary Stagg

The Edge of Forever

Dream Spiral

Sweet Return

Beyond the Horizon

Peter Sterling

Harp Magic

Harp Dreams

Shadow, Mist and Light

New Age

Enya

The Memory of Trees

Paint the Sky with Stars

Watermark

Shepherd Moon

Amartine

A Day Without Rain

Ray Lynch

The Sky of Mind
Deep Breakfast

Here are two of my playlists that I use frequently – a spiritual one and a soothing one. Enjoy!

Kathleen's Spiritual Music Playlist

"Du vilar" by Orphei Drangar

"Forever Young" by Spiritus

"In My Life" by The Secret Pianist

"Yellow" by Scala & Kolacny Brothers

"Ballerina" by Gnomusy

"Sea of Tranquility" by Julius Aston

"Harps" by Heinz Goldblatt

"Ave Maria" by Jonta Lei

"Pleasant Dreams" by Hilary Stagg

"Sounds of Silence" by Mr. and Mrs. Cello

"Lazy Day" by Peter Sterling

"Voice of Angels" by Fiona Joy Hawkins

"First Touch" by Kostia

"Morning Poem" by Andreas Vollenweider

"Heavens Caravan" by Mehdi

"Gemini" by Henrik Janson

"Scarborough Fair/Canticle" by William Ellwood

"Dingle Bay Dream" by Andrew White

"Easy Go" by Henri Seroka

"May It Be" by Sound Haven

"Capri Interlude for Guitar" by Henrik Janson

"High Sierra" by Tim Janis

"Desert Rain" by David Lanz, Paul Sper

"Deep Peace" by Bill Douglas, Ars Nova Singers

"A True Mother's Love" by Back to Earth

"Touched by Love" by Bernward Koch

"Dance of the Clouds" by Origen

"Calling County Clare" by Fiona Joy Hawkins

"Rays of Love" by Mehdi

"Follow Your Heart" by Joe Yamada

"Rio Amazonas" by Oystein Sevag, Lakki Patey

"Prayers Answered" by Medhi

"Alhambra (Prelude)" by Gandaif

"Dakota" by William Elwood

"Africa- Afrika" by Cusco

"Watermark" by Mike Strickland

"Confidently Floating Seaward" by Gandalf

"Skye Boat Song" by Taryn Harbridge

"May the Road Rise Up to Meet You" by Sarah Mathieson

"Hallelujah" by Benny Martin, The Wong Janice

"Hallelujah" by Jeff Buckley

"All You Need is Love" by Simon Wahl

"Ave Maria" by Daughters of Mary

"The Sound of Silence" by 40 Fingers

"Canon in D" by Brooklyn Duo

"Forever Young" by Martin Tellstrom

Kathleen's Soothing Music Playlist

"Fields of Gold" by Katie Melua

"Oh, Danny Boy" by Athol McGregor

"Smile" by Charlie Chaplin, Thomas Beckmann

"Yesterday" by Brandon Mills

"Unchained Melody" by Sonya O'Malley

"Thank You for the Music" by Benny Andersson

"Hallelujah" by Ben Laver

"Walz for Christine" by Stacey Hersh

"Send in the Clowns" by Leonard Bernstein, Natalie Dessay

"Somewhere Over the Rainbow" by Dan Hawkins

"Chitarra Romantica" by Robert Michaels

"Candle in the Wind" by Owen Richards

"Moon River" by Lang Lang, Madeleine Peyroux

"Let It Be Me" by Roberto Dalla Vecchia

"Bach - Prelude No.1" by Martin Bloch

"A Whiter Shade of Pale" by London Symphony Orchestra

"Moon River" by Gustav Lundgren

"Elvira Madigan" by Gheorghe Zamfir

"Moon River" by Cellos

"The Cradle Song" by Catherine Strutt, Chris Duncan

"O Mio Babbino Caro" by Robin Spielberg

"Your Song" by Christopher Phillips

"Vincent (Starry, Starry Night)" by George Skaroulis

"Variations on the Kanon" by George Winston

"Joy" by George Winston

"Cast Your Fate to the Wind" by George Winston

"Si Bheag Si Mhor" by Alex de Grassi

"Hymn" by Liz Story

"Unchained Melody" by Maurice Jarre

"Caribbean Blue" by Enya

"China Roses" by Enya

"Rocket Man" by Fiona Greenly

"Bridge Over Troubled Water" by John Crome

"Blowin' in the Wind" by John Crome

"And I Love Her" by Terri Matheson

END NOTE

Dear Reader,

While this is the end of the book, I want to thank you for walking this path with me. Whether you've read every word or just picked the chapters that speak to your soul, I am deeply grateful for your company on the spiritual journey.

A Spiritual Tool Kit was written with an open heart, total honesty (some may think too honest!), and a prayer that the right people - you are definitely one - have been drawn to this book, who can most benefit from its pages.

If you decide to have this book by your bedside, I want to bring to your attention the chapter on "Self-Love" and the one on "Affirmations." A spiritual path invariably increases our self-esteem and shows us the way to discard negative thinking. But it all takes practice.

I hope this book meets you exactly where you are and perhaps offers a spark for you to start on a spiritual path or guidance to strengthen your spiritual growth and awakening.

With Deepest Gratitude and Much Love,

Kathleen

P.S. I do have one small favor to ask. If you found this book helpful or insightful, I would love it if you could take 60 seconds to leave a review on Amazon.

Your thoughts would be so appreciated and will help me with my future writing.

Also, if you'd like to write me a personal note or question, my email address is kathleenpasley@hotmail.com. Every week, I write an essay that is thought provoking, inspirational and funny with a bit of spirituality thrown in. It's FREE! Once I have your e-mail address, you will receive one every Sunday. Just go to my website at www.kathleenpasley.com. Go to the bottom of any page to sign up. If you like this book, I KNOW you will enjoy my weekly shares!

TESTIMONIALS

Praise for "A Spiritual Tool Kit"

Kathleen Pasley's "A Spiritual Tool Kit" stands out for its raw honesty and vulnerability. Unlike many self-help authors, Kathleen doesn't present a facade of perfection. Instead, she shares her real-life struggles and challenges, making her guidance all the more relatable and accessible. Her book shows that spiritual growth isn't about avoiding difficulties, but about learning to navigate them. Kathleen's willingness to be authentic and share her true self is a breath of fresh air. She's not afraid to explore the tough stuff, and that's what makes her advice so valuable. "A Spiritual Tool Kit" is more than just a book - it's a reflection of Kathleen's real-world experience and wisdom. Her approach is refreshingly honest and down-to-earth. I appreciate how she tackles the complexities of life head-on, offering practical tools for overcoming obstacles. By being her genuine self, Kathleen inspires readers to do the same, making her book a truly unique and impactful read."

Edemir Rossi, Spiritual Healer

Brazil

Kathleen's book, "A Spiritual Tool Kit" contains incredible insights for a spiritual path and honest, invaluable tips and exercises for the seeker. Her writing is always positive, relevant, insightful, uplifting and so honestly down to earth. I recommend her book to many of my clients, family and friends. Because each chapter deals with a different topic, I read and reread her book based on subjects that appeal to me at different times.

Fred Kleiner, Ph.D., Counseling Psychologist
Washington, DC

For years, I have been in a spiritual funk, trying to connect more closely with God, but every morning when I awaken, my thoughts are consumed with anxiety and fear. Kathleen's insights have helped me lessen these feelings and direct my mind toward a faith in a higher power—I am finally realizing that I am worthy of divine love. I am so grateful that she shares her wisdom, insights, and humor. She is truly a godsend.

Anne Austin
Oklahoma

STORIES

(in Order of Their Appearance)

www.ingramcontent.com/pod-product-compliance
Lightning Source LLC
Chambersburg PA
CBHW051201120626
46547CB00012B/1160